Dr. Ace's Guide to
PERSONAL
AND FINANCIAL
FREEDOM

DR. ALBERT "ACE" GOERIG

Dr. Ace's Guide to Personal and Financial Freedom

For information about this title or to order other books and/or electronic media, contact the publisher:
ACG Press
222 Lilly Rd. NE, Olympia, WA. 98506
DoctorAce.com

ISBN: 978-0-9753339-1-4

Printed in the United States of America
Cover and Interior design: 1106 Design

Contents

Disclaimer

Preface

As Americans, we live in one of the greatest countries in the world—we can have an incredible life and retire without worrying about money. Most Americans are stressed over their finances and will probably have to keep on working well beyond the retirement age. This is because the coalition of four (advertising industry, media, merchants and banks) and our financial system was designed to take away our freedom and keep us broke and in debt until we die. In this book, I will show you the secrets of getting out of debt quickly, how to create wealth and personal freedom that works. It does not matter how much you make or what you do; this simple program will help you find the peace and financial freedom in your life that you have always wanted. As a dentist and business and financial coach, I have included stories related to my dental practice, my team members, and my practice-management knowledge. The stories help identify problems and solutions that we find in all personal and business experiences.

Everyone I talk to says they want to have wealth and personal freedom. What I find is that more and more people are in worse financial shape today than ever before. Total US consumer debt currently sits at more than $4 trillion and has increased nearly 21% over the last four years. Total revolving debt is $1.446 trillion and has increased 17% over the last four years. In fact, 96% of Americans are prisoners of debt and are slaves to their monthly payments.

The real problem is that most Americans think that always being in debt is normal. The credit card companies—along with the mortgage companies—have trained you in this belief. They have developed a proven profit system that keeps you in debt for a lifetime, so they can steal half of your life's income. You become their cash cow.

In this book, you will learn how to make more than 100% guaranteed return on your money while watching *all* your debts disappear (even your mortgage) in 5–10 years. How would you like to own everything in your life—your home, your cars, your furniture—everything? How would you like to have no monthly debt payments of any kind, including mortgages, rent, car loans or credit card payments? Once you are debt free, you will have 50% to 70% of your income available, allowing you to work less, have more time with your family and to live the life of your dreams. And the best part is that you can do it using the money you are currently earning. This system works for any income level! More importantly, you will learn how to simplify your life and enjoy work more while creating an incredible relationship with your family. The rewards are many. But most of all, I urge you to enjoy the process.

Dr. Albert C. (Ace) Goerig
Olympia, Washington
May, 2019

Foreword

D r. Ace Goerig is a genius when it comes to unlocking the key to happiness in life! He loves sharing his easy-to-implement secrets of contentment, enthusiasm and living the good life...all at the same time. For decades, he has studied burned-out employers/employees in the workforce. From the CEO/owner to the entry-level employees, workers are simply tired of the noose around their necks called *debt*.

We all know that debt reduction at a fast pace is the key to this thirst for "working because we love it" versus hating for Monday to roll around to go back to the paycheck-to-paycheck existence.

Ace's book outlines exactly what others can do to achieve this outrageous happiness in life. There are several key elements: Live below your means early on; pay yourself first each payday; be the most ethical person you know; hire experts to provide the growth in your business that compounds your net by tens of thousands per month. This not only pays down the debt quickly, but it also allows you to work because you "get to" rather than "have to." That, folks, is pure happiness.

Linda Miles, Founder/CEO Linda Miles & Associates; Founder, Speaking Consulting Network

After providing more than 75 financial articles over the last decade, I count only a precious few authors who provide truly relevant and readable financial information for dentists. John Bogle, Warren Buffett and Bert Malkiel have sold millions of books. I've now added Dr. Albert (Ace) Goerig to that list.

Ace quotes Kendrick (Rick) Mercer in the book's introduction: "Life is a process, not an end; if you don't enjoy the process, you'll hate the end!" Ace provides the most efficient way to become financially free and enjoy every precious moment of your life. He gives you a step-by-step, easy and, frankly, not painful, way to build your dream life with financial security. Overall, this 120-page gem is a must-read for all ages.

Dr. Doug Carlsen

CHAPTER 1

Create an Incredible Life Story

n a May 2017 interview with Charlie Rose, Warren Buffett was asked what gave him his greatest joy. *"That I love going to the office," said Buffett. "It has been my painting for more than fifty years. I get to paint what I want; I own the brush, I own the canvas, and the canvas is unlimited. And that is a pretty nice game, and I get to do it every day with people I like. I don't have to associate with anyone who causes my stomach to turn. If I were in politics, I'd have to smile at a lot of people I'd rather hit. I've got a really good deal, and I am hanging onto it."*

Most of us forget that we have the brush and the canvas, and that we can create our story any way we want. This book will help you through the process.

Creating a New Life Story

We are here on this planet for a relatively brief period, and all we have is from now until the end of our lives. So, how can we make the most of this time?

To live our lives to the fullest, we need to create a new vision or story of what is possible. We all can live the rest of our lives as an exciting adventure. For most of us, because of our cultural context and the lack of training we have received regarding financial matters, it is difficult to set up a guide for reaching financial freedom or even to recognize that our way of relating to money could be very different. However, if we write a story about how we want to live, it is easy to develop and follow a guide to fulfill that story. However, most of us don't know how to develop a coherent and compelling story about financial and personal freedom.

Most Americans want to have more time off to enjoy their family, hobbies and personal time. They are burdened by long-term debt. Many of them are stressed at work and exhausted when they come home. They are unable to see the possibilities that life has to offer. With the right game plan, they could be debt free within 5 to 10 years, work fewer days a year in a drama-free, stress-free office where they work with the people they like. You may not realize it, but you have the canvas, and you have the brush to create the life of your dreams. In the Eagles song "Almost Gone" they sing, *So often times it happens that we live our lives in chains, and we never even know we have the key.* This book was created to help you find the key, to show you the possibilities in your business and personal life and to give you the tools and ideas to create your story. As you go through the book, write down the things you want to change and the steps that you will take to create your new life story. The possibilities are endless.

The best stories are specific *and* flexible—specific in offering a full vision with rich detail, and flexible because life is a process and we are always growing. As new experiences arise, we begin to see things at a deeper level. When situations change, we need to give ourselves permission to change our minds to stay within our own integrity. You can create a beautiful story that incorporates abundance into your life. Having your finances in order will help support your positive story so you can live life fully. However, writing a life story takes great courage, because it involves change. Sometimes you need to change many things to live a free and independent life. In this case, you are called upon to face your fears of confrontation and conflict and to create the life you want. Your story shows the world your intent to change and starts you on your new path. Gandhi was once asked, "What is your message to the world?" He replied, "My life is my message." What is your message to your children?

How to bring abundance into your life

The reason we create positive stories is to let the universe know what we want. I personally believe that we can bring anything—positive or negative—into our lives, depending on our thoughts. This happens by creating a clear, positive vision of exactly what we want and knowing (believing) that it will come about. This could be an increase in referrals, doing more cases or finding the right associate or team member. More than 100 years ago, in his book *The Science of Getting Rich,* Wallace Wattles talked about focusing on what you want and not on what you don't want in your life. We need to put our energies into the creative and not the competitive aspects of life. I never spend any time worrying about what others are doing. Why? Because there is unlimited abundance. If we have the right focus and vision, we can bring whatever we want into our lives. The real fun is helping others create abundance in their lives. I spend little time listening to the negative events in the news, which I cannot control. My real joy and happiness come from relationships with family and in my practice. Abundance always comes when we are thankful for all the gifts and richness that we have in our lives.

A Tale of Two Families (age 25)

Family "A" Earns $72,000 a year.
They have fallen for the scam, and they live big. They buy the big home, expensive cars and other toys to build their ego and try to make themselves happy while continually creating debt and making monthly payments.

By age sixty, they have paid off their mortgage and school loan, but they still have a second mortgage, car payments, credit cards and other debts; they have only $80,000 in their retirement account.

Both parents are working full time and resent going into work because they are working just to make their monthly payments. This is reflected in their relationship with their family and co-workers. They will give 2/3 of their life's earnings to their creditors, including the taxes paid on that income. Along with that, they will have given up their freedom and a life of choice, which will keep them working for many more years because they *have* to—not because they *want* to.

Family "B" earns $72,000 a year.
They live simply—on one salary—and use the other salary to pay off debt early. In eight years, they are debt free, including all credit cards, cars, mortgages and school loans.

At age 33, they have no debt and still live on 1/3 of their income. They now have 60% to 70% of their income to invest for retirement, children's education, vacations or charitable contributions. They have less stress, and one spouse may choose to work part time only—choose to be full-time stay-at-home parents. They work because they *want* to—not because they *have* to. They have more time for family and friends. They now pay cash for all purchases.

Because they have maximized their retirement, Personal Bank and personal investments, at age 60, they have more than $3 million in their retirement and personal investment account.

Using this system, a typical family with $72,000 annual income and $209,000 in total debt would be completely debt free in 5 years and 7 months. This includes owning their home, cars and everything else. Then they can start investing in their retirement, children's education and personal investment account, as will be described in the final chapter.

You Can Become a Millionaire

Here are the lessons from the book *The Millionaire Next Door,* by Thomas Stanley and William Danko. Wealth is not the same as your income. Wealth is what you accumulate (net worth) and not what you spend. Wealth comes from hard work, dedication, planning and self-discipline. Millionaires do not live in upscale neighborhoods or drive fancy cars. A millionaire's goal is to become financially independent, which is much more important than displaying high social status. These financially successful people control their consumption and do not allocate too much money to products and services. Millionaires are frugal; they live not only *below* their means—they live *well* below their means. Most millionaires live in an average home and drive a used car; their children go to public schools. They are married to the same spouse, who is also a conservative spender. Warren Buffett, one of the richest men in the world, has lived in the same modest house for more than sixty years, sent his children to public schools and drives an eight-year-old car.

We all have choices on where we want to spend our money. We could buy a smaller house, go on fewer vacations, buy a smaller car and put more money into investments. Most people do not consciously sit down and consider their choices; instead, they haphazardly spend their money without focus. Until we are debt free, we are restrained by our income, so we need to create a game plan and focus our excess money in order to draw up a guide for personal and financial success.

I used to go fishing each year with my brother on the Kenai Peninsula in Alaska. For $200 a day, we would hire an older fishing guide, named Bob. He had a small (14-foot) Lund boat that we would drag out into the ocean and fish for salmon about 100 yards offshore. When he was not guiding, he would drive a school bus during the rest of the year. His wife worked at the post office, and they lived in a small log cabin near the ocean. They lived very conservatively and ate well on salmon and meat from hunting season. Bob died in 2008 at the age of 87. My brother, who was Bob's attorney, was shocked to find that his investment in a Schwab account was more than $8 million. He had most of his money invested in no-load index funds, as described in the final chapter. This program can make anyone with the right commitment a millionaire.

CHAPTER 2

The Fastest Way to Become Financially Free

When all investments are put into perspective, the best returns are from paying off debt and increasing your business profitability. These choices can give you a return of more than 100%. Below are the past ten years' average returns on various investments.

- **Home:** 0–5%. According to Zillow, while home prices have appreciated nationally at an average annual rate between 3% and 5%, depending on the index used for the calculation, home-value appreciation in different metro areas can appreciate at markedly different rates than the national average. Over time, home values grew about 0% after inflation. Plan on spending 5% of the value of the home to buy it, 10% to sell it and 1% to 2% a year to maintain it.

- **Average actively managed fund investment:** 2.6%. According to *Forbes* ("Why the Average Investor's Investment Return Is So Low," Sean Hanlon, Apr 24, 2014), the average investor in a blend of equities and fixed-income mutual funds has earned only a 2.6% or less net annualized rate of return for the ten-year period.

- **Inflation:** The current inflation rate reported by the US Department of Labor for the United States is 2.8% for the 12 months that ended May 2018. Remember that a 3% inflation reduces your 10% stock return to only 7%. But it also can reduce your 2% return on bonds to a negative 1%.

- **Short-term Bonds:** Over the past five years, bonds have returned only 1.4% annually.

- **Personal Bank (infinite banking concept):** Over the past 30 years it has provided a **guaranteed tax-free** return of 4% to 5% (see chapter 6 and go to personalbank4u.com).

- **S&P 500:** The most recent 15-year return on this index is 8.8%, although the average over the past 50 years has been around 7%.

- **No-fee investing saves you up to 70% more on your investment returns. This can be done by investing on your own, which is well described in this book.** When you pay 1% to 4% in fees to financial advisors, brokers or mutual fund companies that actively manage your investments, it could cost you 70% of your return, making you work 10 to 15 years longer before you can retire. If you pay fees of 3% and your investments return only 4%, you get 25% of the return, and your broker and mutual fund get 75% of the return. What happens when the return is only 2%? Your commissioned broker's mantra is "Heads I win, tails you lose." Learn to invest on your own. This book will show you how.

- **Paying off debt:** Up to 500% (5×) return.

- **Investing in yourself or your business:** Up to 100% increase in return on investment.

You will see how the power of paying off debt can give you a guaranteed return of more than 100% without risk or tax consequence. Everyone needs to focus on what produces the greatest returns. If you execute this game plan right, then you will have more money than you will ever need, which you can trade in for time, freedom and choices. Investing in the stock market is not a way to make you rich quickly. It is a way to allow your money to compound over time to provide a very comfortable retirement. I will show you the best strategies to safely get the highest returns investing by yourself, without paying the extraordinarily high fees and commissions of financial advisors, brokers and mutual fund companies, where they can take 70% of your retirement returns.

When this strategy is implemented correctly, you will never have to touch the money you have in the market. Remember that paying off debt first while you increase your income provides the highest returns, with much more predictability than anything you could do by investing in the market.

Freedom Facts

The fastest way to become financially free is to pay off all debts before you put money anywhere else. **The advantages to paying off debt first are:**

1. Easiest and simplest to do and understand.

2. Can make more than 100% return on your money, guaranteed, without risk or tax consequence.

3. Can be done automatically, right out of your bank account.

4. Changes you from a spender into a saver.

5. You can now invest more into higher-return stocks like the S&P 500 index fund because your paid-off home and business act like a long-term, inflation-adjusted bond. The 20% of your income that you were using to pay off your mortgage now becomes a bond-like investment, getting 20% return on your paid-off home.

6. Once debt free, you have three times the amount of disposable income (previously, 2/3 of your disposable income was paid toward debt) to spend on investments and enjoying life.

One of the biggest misconceptions that keeps you in debt which is per-petuated by banks and accountants is that you should not pay off your house early, because when you have a mortgage, you can write off the interest rate on your taxes. This allows the banks to continue to get a large amount of interest from using your money. If you are in the 28% federal income tax bracket and itemize your deductions, you pay one dollar of mortgage interest and save $.28 in taxes. This means you lose $.72 of one dollar to save $.28 in taxes.

Let's look at this closely: In 2018, an average American couple who pays $10,000 a year in interest on their home loan has the choice of either taking the standard deduction of $24,000 or itemizing their return and taking the $10,000 tax write-off. When they itemize, they are unable to take the standard deduction of $24,000 and have an overall loss of $14,000 in standard deduction. The biggest loss is in the interest you paid the bank, which could range more than 200%.

Please consider a $310,000 mortgage at 4.5% for thirty years. Below, you can see that, of the first year's loan payment of $18,849, only $5,001 goes to principal, but $13,848 goes to interest, which is lost forever to you. See Figure 1 below. ***This is a 277% loan, not a 4.5% loan.***

In the 28% tax bracket, you had to earn around $17,724 and pay taxes on that to get the $13,847 to give to the bank as interest payments, which makes it a 354% loan. If you pay an additional principal payment of $5,231, you would eliminate one year's payment and save $13,618 in interest; you will have made a 354% return on your money, guaranteed, without risk or any tax consequence (see below).

Year	Interest	Principal	Balance
2019	$13,848	$5,001	$304,999
2020	$13,618	$5,231	$299,768
2021	$13,378	$5,471	$294,297
2022	$13,126	$5,722	$288,575
2023	$12,863	$5,985	$282,590
Total (after 5 years)	**$68,833**	**$27,410**	**$282,590**

Figure 1

The reality: Over the next five years, you would have paid $96,243 in loan payments, and only $27,410 would have gone to pay off the loan. You must understand that the interest is always the highest at the beginning of the loan, and for the first ten years of a 30-year loan, the interest paid will always be more than 100%. Always take advantage of this guaranteed high return. **The bottom line: you invested $5001 and made $13,848, which is a guaranteed 277% return without risk. With this great return, why would anyone not use the money in their savings (earning only less than 1%) to pay off their home? You should also cash out any non-tax-deferred stocks and pay off debts.**

When we have debt, saving money is an encoded trap that keeps us poor. In the above example, if you have $100,000 in your savings or non-tax-deferred investments, the best, safest and highest return on that money is to pay off debt. Paying $100,000 toward the $310,000 home mortgage would drop your mortgage to $210,000 and save you $121,360 in interest payments—while paying off 13 years of the mortgage. Compare this $121,360 made by paying off debt to the $1,500 you would get with an after-tax return of 1.5% in a 2% bank CD on that same $100,000. You must see the $100,000 put into the house as a high-return, safe, long-term, inflation-adjusted bond that is always available to you through lines of credit or second mortgages. Once the home is paid off, the money used for mortgage payments becomes a constant source of available cash flow. It is like getting money from a bond.

Remember, focus on paying off debt before you put your money anywhere else. Once you are debt free, I will show you specific investment strategies that provide safe and predictable results. Most people can be debt free within five to ten years using this guide.

Debt Is the Devil

It's all about net worth. Our net worth is the total of all our assets, including our investments, bank accounts and real estate, minus our debts. Paying off debt increases your net worth (wealth) and provides an asset that you can use in emergencies as loan collateral. Paying off debt is a conservative investment strategy. Don't be happy about having more tax deductions, especially when you can't write them off due to the high standard deduction. This is how the government and the banks keep you in debt and in servitude.

There is no good debt—there is only bad debt. All debt is bad, bad, bad! Debt keeps you imprisoned and prevents you from living a life of freedom, independence and choice. Being overburdened with financial responsibilities increases your stress; it can damage important and satisfying personal relationships and even lead to divorce, which could cost half of what you own. By changing your spending and saving habits one step at a time, you can regain control of your life. You now know what interest payments really cost you and what to do to change your spending habits.

In John Cummuta's excellent audiobook and manual *Transforming Debt into Wealth,* he states, "Every time you make a purchase on credit, you need to consider not just the price you're paying for the product but the price plus interest—plus how much that money could have earned you as an investment."

US households now owe $13.15 trillion in total debt, and about $931 billion of that is credit card debt, according to NerdWallet's 2017 American Household Credit Card Debt Study, along with its newly issued quarterly figures. In 2017, the average family's collective balance on all credit cards was more than $16,000. If the family makes just the minimum payment, it would take them thirty-seven and a half years to pay off the balance; over that time, they would make total payments of more than $43,000, of which $26,000 would be interest. This is the same as someone saying to you, "I will lend you $16,000, and you will pay me back $43,000." If you were to invest the same $26,000 in an individual retirement account (IRA), it would grow to $284,329 over 30 years at 8% interest. We have spent tomorrow's money already and are making payments on it.

With each debt, the interest you pay puts you on the wrong side of the compound-interest equation. It's important to realize that you are going to make a finite amount of money in your life. If you give too much of it away in interest payments and impulse buying, there will not be enough money left over for you to retire comfortably. You can take two basic approaches with your money: you can spend it on things that don't add meaning to your life and stay in debt and eat cat food in your retirement years, or you can build your financial future now by paying off debt early and retire early in style. Every dollar you consume now brings you one dollar of value, but every dollar you use to pay off debt can bring you five to twenty times that amount in your retirement years, allowing you to retire ten to twenty years earlier. Reducing spending and paying off debt will eliminate money problems, improve relationships and improve your health by reducing stress. And it will serve as a shining example for your children about what is possible.

How would it feel to be out of debt and own your home free and clear, with utilities, taxes and food as your only real expenses? This is possible for everyone if they're following a clear guide. Most people can pay off all of their credit card debt in one year and their car in the second year. By the third year, they're making extra payments toward their mortgage. Most people can be totally debt free within five to ten years and thereby eliminate payments on student loans, home loans and business debts.

When you become debt free, there is no need to worry about your credit report, because you pay cash for all your purchases. *The ability to obtain credit is what got you into trouble in the first place.* The idea that you need to build up your credit by borrowing is an illusion that keeps you in debt. Once you become debt free, no one owns you, and this is true freedom.

Steps to Eliminate Debt

Eliminating debt is a crucial first step in my game plan. The only debt that is reasonable to incur is for the purchase of very large items, such as your house, your education or your car. Never go into debt for anything else, especially not for consumable items.

I can't state it any more clearly: consumption debt is bad, bad, bad and bad. The best strategy is to spend less than you make and to save a substantial amount of your money. Then you can consume with saved dollars. Most families in America are imprinted to use their credit cards and consume, whether they have the money to pay for something or not. If you do this, you typically pay high interest rates; this is not an effective way to manage your money. It is not a bad idea to start cutting up all credit cards except one that you may need. Use a debit card instead of a credit card. **For a step-by-step approach to eliminating debt quickly, we can use the debt-elimination worksheet in Appendix B.**

CHAPTER 3

Ideas on How to Find and Make More Money

An extra job becomes the rocket booster to accelerate your debt reduction.

- ✓ Make more at your job, and put it toward debt.

- ✓ Do consulting work from home.

- ✓ Set up an eBay account and business.

- ✓ Learn how to create an online business at home. Go to the resource section at Doctorace.com and click the link to the Online Business Academy. Go to clients at their home (bookkeepers or computer experts).

- ✓ Teach college at night.

- ✓ Check out internet on "work-at-home jobs" (watch out for scams).

- ✓ Multilevel marketing (e.g., Mary Kay) (watch out for scams).

- ✓ Go back to school to give you opportunities for a higher-paying job. Make all efforts to pay off the school loans early.

- ✓ With an extra job, you could be debt free three years earlier.

Other ideas for finding extra money:

✓ Stop funding retirement until debt free, except for matching contributions.

✓ Get rid of your emergency fund. Once your credit card is paid, it becomes your emergency fund.

✓ Evaluate/reduce holiday gift giving.

✓ Check bank/credit card statement.

✓ Stop smoking.

✓ Properly maintain your home and car.

✓ Never buy a brand-new car until debt free.

✓ Never finance beyond 36 months.

✓ Take advantage of "cheap," meaningful vacations.

✓ ‚Don't buy tools/boats you don't often use—rent or borrow them.

✓ Conserve utility usage.

✓ Avoid "Retail Therapy."

✓ Learn to say "No" to kids.

✓ Think like Warren Buffet, and send your children to public grade schools and high schools instead of private schools.

✓ Stop funding your children's education. Let them pay for college.

✓ Apply all bonuses and pay raises toward debt.

✓ Eliminate private mortgage insurance (PMI) by paying down the mortgage balance to 80% of the home's original appraised value.

✓ Evaluate your real insurance needs.

✓ Auto insurance: get higher deductibles.

✓ Personal-liability insurance.

✓ Medical insurance.

✓ Get higher deductibles.

✓ Get an umbrella attachment.

✓ Never buy extended warranties.

✓ Use coupons (retailmenot.com, Joinhoney.com).

✓ Stop getting tax refunds.

✓ Spare-change jar.

✓ Have only a cell phone.

✓ Minimize dining out. Move to brown-bag lunches.

✓ Simplified lifestyle.

✓ Entertainment.

✓ Movies.

✓ Get rid of cable.

✓ Shop at outlet malls/Goodwill.

✓ See if you can refinance your home at a lower rate without fees through Quicken loans or a local bank.

✓ Buy a duplex, and live in one side; use your renter payment to double your monthly mortgage payments. Look at prebuilt homes as a starter home.

One of the fastest ways to become debt free is to move to a cheaper location. The average US home costs $149,900. It is a lot easier to get out of debt if you buy your home in a location where the home prices are low, such as in Atlanta, Georgia, where an average home is $88,400, compared to San Jose, California, where the average home is $530,000.

This is *not* a no-spending plan; it is a managed-spending plan. I am not saying you can't spend any money on the things you want. But I *do* want you to be aware of the impact that each expenditure has on your ability to build your wealth. Most people can easily spend and live on half the amount they normally spend.

Financial freedom is just a mindset and a numbers game. Once your plan is implemented, you will be debt free in 5 to 7 years. You now can stop worrying and focus on each day and enjoy the process of life.

CHAPTER 4

Learn How to Invest
Safely and Simply

O nce you are debt free, you need to know the safest places to invest your
money, without high risk and without management fees. This part
of the book will give you a specific game plan to reach your investment goals. The greatest return on your investment always comes first from
paying off debt and by making more money at your work or business. The
next safest and guaranteed investment is in the creation of a Personal Bank.
This is a specialized, whole-life insurance policy that gives you a consistent
tax-free return. This is discussed in Chapter 5. Investing in the stock market
may provide a higher nonguaranteed taxable return but is more volatile, with
higher risks. The return can be significantly increased when you learn to
eliminate fees by investing on your own through a company such as Schwab
or Vanguard, which I will discuss below.

Disclaimer

I have found the following investment information to be helpful. I am not engaged in rendering professional services. If you require personal assistance or advice, seek a competent professional. I specifically disclaim any responsibility for any loss, liability or risk, personal or otherwise, which is incurred directly or indirectly from the use and application of the contents of this book.

Many individuals get confused with investing and do not understand how easy it is to invest on their own through a company like Schwab or Vanguard. That is why they are so vulnerable to investment schemes and high-fee advisors and brokers. In this chapter, I will give you the secret to simple investing. More in-depth detail will be found in Chapter 5.

When I first started coaching dentists and their employees, I knew debt reduction and financial freedom were important. I also knew that people could achieve financial freedom easily. I had grand dreams about how I could make a big difference in people's lives. I developed the Financial Freedom Guide, through which they could accumulate gigantic amounts of money, and I showed them a sure and safe path to financial freedom. I had the illusion that, in this way, I could help my clients commit themselves to a safe economic pathway and change their lives.

I soon became discouraged, because many of my clients and their CPAs, brokers and financial advisors made a mess out of my finely designed plans. Instead of paying off debt, these "helpers" encouraged my clients to take their money and buy risky stocks, hedge funds, annuities and speculative real estate. They put their clients' assets into actively managed mutual funds that took 3% to 4% of their return for themselves, resulting in a 60% to 70% loss of return that could have been made for my clients. The losses were in the millions of dollars in my clients' investment portfolios, thus preventing geometric progression of their retirement plans and undermining my advice.

We seem to have an infinite capacity to stress ourselves, especially when it comes to money. To a large degree, this comes from greed and ego. I knew one individual who took his entire retirement plan of $300,000 and put it into a limited partnership. He did not really understand the potential risks and rewards, and he had no control over them. Within one year, he'd lost his entire retirement nest egg that had taken him twenty years to earn. I know a very smart and skilled doctor who got involved in a "Bernie Madoff"-type scheme and lost his entire savings of $1.3 million that had taken him twenty years to accumulate.

I teach from my own life experiences and have probably made every financial mistake in the book, including day trading, buying an oil well over the phone for $5,000 that disappeared in a few months, buying timeshares and buying land where I was never going to live. From my many life experiences, financial misadventures and my work as a coach and financial mentor, I have developed a consistent philosophy and a guide to investing that can work for anyone.

In my money context, I want to reach financial freedom as safely and quickly as I can. People have a wide range of economic strategies. Some spread out their money and lose it by placing it into various so-called "investments" such as risky stocks, hedge funds and speculative real estate, commodities, day trading and limited partnerships, hoping they will strike it rich. These strategies are not efficient or reliable. Another strategy some people use is to reduce the amount of taxes they pay. Personally, I know that the more taxes I pay, the more money I am making. Americans have a history of hating taxes. One of the things that pushed us into the American Revolution was taxation by England without representation. So, it's not surprising that one popular economic program revolves around avoiding taxes. In the 1970s and 1980s, there were tax shelters that were really taxes in disguise.

Some people are so busy avoiding taxes that they lose sight of the goal of financial freedom. Some people buy larger houses than they need so they'll have more interest to write off on their taxes. Saving money on taxes is foolish if it costs more money than it saves.

Everyone in this country could become financially free if they spent less than they made, or made more than they spent, got out of debt and invested the difference in safe, liquid assets. If numbers and the idea of self-investing confuse you, this next paragraph will summarize all you need to know about successful investing. For a more in-depth understanding of investing, risk management and investment options, go to chapter 5 and 6.

Dr. Ace's Simple Investing Summary

Make more money at work or in your business, and focus all money toward debt reduction. Once you are debt free, your assets, such as your business or your home, act like a long-term, inflation-adjusted bond that can be used to obtain a line of credit or a source of income. The next safest form of investment is creating a Personal Bank. This is a specially designed, dividend-paying whole-life insurance policy, where most of your premiums go into a rider that accelerates the growth of your equity and cash value in the policy. To learn more about infinite banking and how to create your own Personal Bank, go to chapter 6 and PersonalBank4u.com. The modified policy reduces the commission the advisor receives by 70% to 85%, and you will have up to 90 times more cash value, especially in the early years, than with a traditional whole-life policy. Because of the lower commission, most insurance agents do not offer this policy. To find an agent who knows how to design a high cash value policy with the right companies, check out the links at Doctorace. com. These policies offer guaranteed tax-free growth and safety for your principal investment regardless of the ups and downs of the stock market or the economy. You will be able to use it as a financial-management tool right from the beginning. This policy provides you tax-free access to your money for purchases, disability income or tax-free money for your retirement years, giving you guaranteed growth. It provides peace of mind and an income-tax-free legacy that you can pass on to your loved ones and/or favorite charities without going through probate. This is one of the safest, no-risk investments and acts like a pension or long-term bond. Because of their safety, consistent returns and the liquidity, most major banks have cash value life insurance position as the top asset on their balance sheet.

Once you are debt-free and have a Personal Bank for security, you can put additional money into a riskier environment, such as the stock market. To maximize your returns, learn to invest yourself in the US market without paying advisors or mutual fund companies 1% to 4% of your return, resulting in a 50% to 70% loss of your overall investment return. Today, it is easy to invest on your own and eliminate these advisory and mutual-fund fees. In this book, you will see how easy it is to create a Schwab account or a Vanguard account and learn to invest safely and predictably on your own. Both companies have great salaried advisors who will teach you how to invest on your own, step by step. Many of the "helpers" (brokers, mutual-fund companies and financial advisors that you may have now) provide complicated investing strategies with multiple investment choices or investment theories such as Modern Portfolio Design, so you will think that investing is complicated and too hard for you to do alone. That is why investors are tricked into paying them high fees, even though their returns are less than the S&P 500 or US stock index. William Bernstein said, *"You are engaged in a life-and-death struggle with the financial service industry. Every dollar in fees, expenses, and spreads you pay them comes directly out of your pocket. Act as if every broker, insurance salesman, mutual fund salesperson and financial advisor you encounter is a hardened criminal, and stick to low-cost index funds, and you'll just do fine."* So, don't fall for that scam.

I was talking with a good friend who had just recently married a beautiful lady whose husband had died three years before. She related a story of a broker she went to for help with her investments, which she knew little about. She was still dazed and confused from her loss and took all the funds she had gathered from selling homes, cars, business and closing accounts. In December 2012, she gave the broker all her assets and asked him to "Manage this, be conservative, thank you."

He immediately placed her in an "actively managed account" and charged a 1% "wrap fee" annually. *Plus,* there were fees inside the account, e.g., front-end loads on mutual funds and high annual fees on mutual funds! In mid-2014, my friend and his new wife tried to get a handle on her returns, fees and commissions. They asked the financial advisor three questions: What was the return in the managed portfolio in 2013? (Answer … +5%.) What was the S&P 500 return for 2013? (The answer was … +32.31%.) The third question was: How much were the total fees charged to manage the portfolio for 2013? (The answer … $28,000!) This story is not uncommon in the brokerage world and demonstrates why we need to understand the simple concepts of investing safely.

If you are with a financial advisor or a mutual-fund company that is charging you more than $1,000 to $4,000 per year, you are paying too much and should transfer assets to Schwab or Vanguard into a low-cost index fund.

Remember that a 1% to 2% fee could reduce your retirement assets to the point that you will have to work another ten to fifteen years. I personally use Schwab because they are open 24 hours a day, seven days a week, have no minimum balance to open an account, and all trades within their funds and ETFs are free. All other trades, no matter what the amount, are $4.95. This is a great place to put your children's money: Roth IRAs. Both Schwab and Vanguard make it very easy for you to transfer assets from your overpriced mutual-fund company and advisor into their company.

Most of us do not like confrontation with our past advisor when we try to transfer our assets. It becomes very easy when you call a Schwab representative and fill out the forms to have your assets automatically transferred into your new Schwab account. You don't even need to talk to your former advisor. To avoid the higher fees in your old company when you sell a stock or heavily loaded mutual fund, have the assets transferred to Schwab first; then sell them for only $4.95. When you transfer your account, ask for twenty free trades for opening your account. There may be a few mutual funds that they cannot transfer over; those will need to be sold into cash at your former brokerage house.

Many advisors recommend diversifying into US stocks, international stocks and bonds. This will depend on your risk tolerance and other factors. Chapter 5 will help you narrow your list of best individual asset allocation between bonds and stocks. Because you will be debt free, produce an income and have a Personal Bank, you can take more risk and have most of your portfolio in stocks such as the low-cost S&P 500 or total US stock market index mutual fund or ETF as described below. Then you're done.

Just buy the US market, which means the S&P 500 or the total US stock market mutual fund. Because there are always ups and downs in the market, wait until after there is at least a 10% drop in the market before you buy. If the market drops more, continue to buy. You can buy the Schwab S&P 500 index mutual fund (ticker symbol SWPPX) at the expense ratio of 0.03%, or the Vanguard 500 index mutual fund (ticker symbol VFIAX) with an expense ratio of 0.04%, both returning an average annual return over a ten-year period of about 15.3% and an average annual return over a fifteen-year period of 8.8%. Or you can buy Schwab US Broad Total Market index mutual fund (ticker symbol SWTSX) at the expense ratio of 0.03%, or the Vanguard Total Stock Market Index mutual fund (ticker symbol VTSAX with an expense ratio of 0.04%, both returning an average annual return over a ten-year period of 15.3% and an average annual return over a fifteen-year period of 9%.

Each month, automatically transfer a set amount of money from your bank to your Schwab or Vanguard money market account. Always stay in the market, and never sell, especially when the market drops: this is the time to buy more index funds, not sell. On April 29, 2019, the markets again are moving up to all-time highs. This may not be the time to buy into the market. Remember the adage about buy low and sell high. I personally like to keep my money and the Schwab money market account and take advantage of market drops throughout the year that are greater than 10%, as occurred in 2018, and buy the S&P 500 or the US stock market index using your money market account. Stop listening to the news and what's happening in the economy or the market. This is just noise. Don't even open your monthly investment statements. Check once a year in December when you give the statements to your CPA. If you want to have a 401(k) plan for your office, go to America's Best 401(k) plan. That's it—you're done. Now enjoy your life.

I know that an all-stock portfolio such as the S&P 500 index fund sounds risky, but because of recent low interest rates, the ten years' total bond funds returns averaged 3.4%, international stocks averaged 6.6%, and the S&P 500 averaged 13%. History has always shown that the S&P 500 index has had a consistently higher return over time as compared to bonds and international stocks. This is the fastest way to become financially free. If you want high returns, you are going to invest in stocks (S&P 500) and occasionally experience losses in the market—but only if you sell—and if you want safety, you're going to invest in bonds and endure low returns.

When you are working, your steady income is like having a bond portion in your portfolio. Also, your paid-off debt, such as your home, your business and your building, are like a long-term, inflation-adjusted bond that is not affected by market corrections. The Personal Bank has guaranteed growth 4% to 6% and cash value that you can borrow from if necessary. This is the best place to store your money. Your Personal Bank provide a source of emergency money and is just like a home-equity loans or lines of credit. Your income is like an inflation-protected asset, which allows you to invest in other investment that give you a greater return such as equities (S&P 500) or real estate.

We are not smart enough to beat the market, but all we need to do is match the market. Long term, you may never need to touch your retirement principle and live off the dividends and interest. If you love what you do, you can easily fund your lifestyle by working part time. If you retire completely, you will be debt free and have your Social Security, tax-free money from your Personal Bank, money from the sale of your business, your 401(k) distributions, dividends from your stocks and possibly rental income, allowing you to continue to invest in equities. Social Security is like owning a big inflation-indexed bond delivering a stream of income that rises with inflation. Chapter 6 will help you better understand the different investment options and how to invest in the market on your own. You will also find recommendations for safer (low-return) investments for those who are more fearful about downturns in the market. Each of us knows how much risk we can take so that we can sleep well at night. Do the pillow test. If you lay your head on your pillow at night and you are thinking about your stock portfolio, then reduce the amount of equities in your portfolio until you can fall asleep peacefully.

At the beginning of the annual Berkshire Hathaway meeting in 2018, Warren Buffett wanted to share an important lesson with its shareholders. I will summarize what he said: *"Let's look back to 1942, when I bought my first stock and all the things that have happened since that time. We have had fourteen presidents, seven Republicans and seven Democrats. We had world wars, 9/11, Cuban missile crisis, and all kinds of terrible events that affected the market. But the best single thing you could have done on March 11, 1942, when I bought my first stock was to buy an index fund* (Buffett specifically mentioned the S&P 500 index fund) *and never, ever look at another headline. Just like you would have bought a farm and let the tenant farmer run it for you and never sell it. If you had put in $10,000 in an index fund at that time and reinvested the dividends, you would have $51 million today in 2018.*

If you took the same $10,000 and bought 300 ounces of gold, you would have only about $400,000 today. Gold does not produce anything, but businesses do. All you needed to do was to believe America would win the war and America would progress as it has ever since 1776. As America moves forward, American business moves forward. You didn't have to worry what stock to buy or what day *to get in or out of the market or what the Federal Reserve would say. You just had to know that America works!"*

Investment Vehicles for Pension Plans and IRAs

Once you are debt free and have a Personal Bank, I highly recommend that you take advantage of the various tax-deferred IRAs, pension and 401(k) plans that are available to you. In his recent book *Unshakeable,* Tony Robbins spent a lot of time talking about how most companies that provide and manage 401(k) plans are ripping off the participants and owners of the plan. These plans are loaded with expensive mutual funds, excessive administrative expenses and fat commissions to the brokers who sell the plan. In contrast, America's Best 401(k) is a company that offers only inexpensive index funds from firms such as Vanguard and dimensional fund advisors. Tom Zgainer, CEO of the company, charges only one fee, with no markups or hidden costs. It is a full, bundled solution that eliminates brokers, commissions and highly paid middlemen. He recommends investing with America's Best 401(k) to get the best returns at the lowest cost.

In addition to 401(k) plans, AB 401(k) also manages Cash Balance (CB) plans. When paired with a 401(k), the CB plan allows for rapidly accelerated contributions while at the same time significantly reducing tax liability. These paired plans will generally work better with individuals older than 40 than with younger employees. I recommend you go to the website and use the company's free online Fee Checker tool at www.ShowMeTheFees.com. I have sent many of my clients to compare the fees at America's Best, and they have all moved their plans.

As an example, one of my clients who had about $1.4 million in her plan and added about $100,000 each year did a fee comparison. America's Best 401(k) total annual investment-related fees were 0.5%, compared to 1.73% in her original plan. If both plans got a 7% return over the next twenty years, the 1.23% difference in fees would have cost her $1.7 million in lost retirement savings for herself and her employees. To look at this in another way, **because of that 1.23% fee, which would have resulted in a $1.7 million personal financial loss,** she and her employees would have to work for another ten years before retiring. Over a 30-year period, the loss would be $4.93 million. How many more years do you have to work with a 3% advisor or actively managed fund fee? By eliminating the fees, it allows you to buy back the one thing that is limited in your life, which is your time on this planet. This is why it is essential that you compare plans.

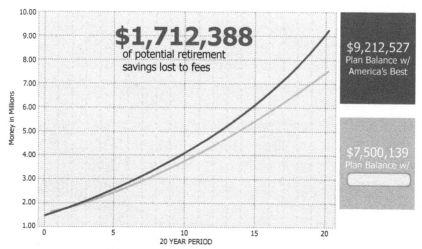

IMPACT OF FEES ON BALANCE OVER TIME

Ending Balance	America's Best	Other plan	Increased Retirement Savings
Year 1	$1,597,054.67	$1,577,312.19	$19,742
Year 5	$2,526,285.66	$2,387,107.28	$139,178
Year 10	$4,083,417.55	$3,669,528.16	$413,889
Year 20	$9,212,526.80	$7,500,138.91	$1,712,388

Figure 7

Estate Planning and Asset Protection Checklist

More than 30% of my clients do not have a will, power of attorney or trust. Without these items, there is a great possibility that if something happens to them and their spouse, their drunken brother will take over all the money, spend it and throw their kids out on the street. Think about it. Without a revocable living trust, their estate will go into probate, which makes all their assets public and is very expensive and emotionally draining to their heirs. It could take years before the estate is settled, thus depleting much of the estate's assets.

I was working with a thirty-four-year-old dentist who had a very nice practice, a little girl, and one more child on the way. I told him to go to his local attorney and get these estate-planning documents drawn up. He said he would. Six months later, he was coming with his wife and team to one of my seminars in Seattle. During the flight, the plane had a landing-gear issue, and they thought they would have to make a crash landing in Seattle. Fortunately, they got the gear down and landed safely. At the meeting, I asked him, "Don't you feel better now that you have your asset-protection plan in place?" He sheepishly said, "I will get those things done as soon as I get back."

Find a local attorney, and get these things done now:

- Durable power of attorney for healthcare

- Durable power of attorney for finances

- Living will

- Standard will

- Revocable living trust

- Irrevocable trust

For a less-expensive approach, you can also go to LegalZoom and set up one for as little as $250 with the help of its attorneys. http://www.legalzoom.com/living-trusts/living-trusts-overview.html

Make sure to update beneficiaries on all your banking and investment accounts. The beneficiaries get first claim, and those listed on the will are secondary. Also go to DoctorAce.com and download a free document locator to let others know where important documents are and the passwords to all your Internet sites, such as banking and investments. Make sure someone you trust is available in case a worst-case scenario happens to you.

Recommended additional reading:

Dahle, James M., MD *The White Coat Investor: A Doctor's Guide to Personal Finance and Investing.* The White Coat Investor LLC. 2014.

https://www.whitecoatinvestor.com/introduction-to-estate-planning/

https://www.thebalance.com/why-beneficiary-designations-override-your-will-2388824

Life Insurance. In the past, I was a big fan of cheap term insurance, as compared to a standard, whole-life insurance policy. However, I have recently realized the power of having permanent whole-life insurance that can be modified to create your own Personal Bank as a high yield tax-free saving asset. This can be one of the best and safest places to save your money without risk while receiving consistent, predictable returns and can be a legacy to your family. Most insurance salesmen are unaware of this type of policy, so for more information on the Personal Bank go to personalbank4U.com.

Disability insurance. I recommend that you go to the Eagleston financial group to evaluate all your insurance needs, such as disability insurance. (http://eaglestonfinancialgroup.com/). I have worked with them for many years, and they are extremely helpful and very honest.

Should you buy or rent a home? Bottom line: do not purchase a home until you are debt free and you have at least a 20% down payment. In 2019, the median home-listing price in the US is nearly $280,000, according to Zillow, that varies by state. The average American moves every 7 years. By then, only 12% of the home is paid off. Then they get a new mortgage, starting all over again at 100%. With a $280,000 mortgage, they have paid $34,257 toward their mortgage and lost $90,569 to the bank in interest during those seven years. They also paid an additional 6% in sales commission ($16,800), $10,000 in home improvements, plus $4,000 in closing costs. The bottom line is that there was no increase in their net worth, and they will never, ever get out of debt.

If they stay in the home and choose to pay back the original $280,000 loan at 4.9 % over the next 30 years, they will pay the $280,000 home price plus the $254,972 in interest, which equals $534,972 in after-tax money. I recommend that you never carry a mortgage larger than **2½ times** your gross income, and you should not spend more than 16% of your gross income on housing, including your mortgage payment, utilities, property tax, insurance and maintenance. Buy a home that is just large enough for your family and one you can afford to pay off in seven to ten years. Make sure you get a mortgage that has no penalty or fee for paying it off early. If you pay off the

$280,000 home in seven years, you will save $51,225 in interest and have an additional $203,647 to invest in your retirement plan.

Remember: when buying a home over 30 years, most of the mortgage payments initially go to interest, and very little goes to the principal (ownership) to pay off the home. For the first 15 years, it is just like renting, except you have all the additional property taxes, maintenance and homeowner's insurance. Beyond that, in most cases, you **can't** write off the interest on your taxes because they are less than the standard deduction. You are much better off renting until you have a 20% down payment (to eliminate the need for private mortgage insurance) and can plan to pay off the house in seven to ten years. Focus all excess money on those payments, and don't dilute your extra money by paying into your child's college fund or into your retirement unless it's matched by your employer. Once debt free, you can pay cash for your child's college and other retirement plans. When you buy a home, you have real estate in your portfolio, and it becomes a form of forced savings, just like a long-term, inflation-adjusted bond. Once paid off, the money that went to your mortgage payment now becomes like long-term dividends, which can be invested more aggressively into the S&P 500 or total US stock market. Your paid-off home also becomes a safety net from which equity can be used in emergencies through home-equity loans.

Unlike the dividends and interest from your investments, you don't have to pay taxes on input rent (the past monthly mortgage or rent payment). This tax-free benefit is on top of the better-known tax breaks that home ownership enjoys, including the ability to take a tax deduction on the mortgage interest and property taxes and to avoid capital-gains tax on a big chunk of the profit when selling a home. In addition, when the market drops, you just don't go out and sell your home, like many investors do with their stocks.

The choice between buying a home and renting is among the biggest financial decisions that many adults make. I would recommend renting if you do not plan to live in the house for longer than seven years. Here is a link to a calculator that uses the most important costs associated with buying a house and computes the equivalent monthly rent. https://www.nytimes.com/interactive/2014/upshot/buy-rent-calculator.html

Get rid of private mortgage insurance (PMI). If you did not have a 20% down payment when you purchased your house, you had to buy PMI, or private mortgage insurance. This is very expensive and can cost you up to 1% of the loan amount annually. A $400,000 house will require $4,000 a year in insurance payments, or $333 in monthly payments. In accordance with the Homeowners Protection Act of 1998, your lender must terminate PMI on the date your loan balance is scheduled to reach 78% of the original value of your home (in other words, when your equity reaches 22%, provided you are current on your mortgage payments). Ask your lender to cancel your PMI when you have paid down the mortgage balance to 80% of the home's original appraised value. You might have to write your lender a cancellation letter for the PMI. Accelerate your payments as fast as you can to eliminate the PMI, and, once you've done this, you'll have an additional $333 a month to pay off your home early. https://www.investopedia.com/mortgage/insurance/how-get-rid-pmi/

Financial Myths and Mistakes

Over the years, we have been imprinted with financial myths. Once we look closely at them, we realize how they are wrong and keep us from reaching our financial goals. Below, I will address a few of these beliefs and recommend you see them for what they are: myths.

- **Myth 1: Good debt versus bad debt.** Some people say that your house or your business is good debt. But all debt is bad and sucks the life out of your financial world. We must remember that debt is the devil! Get rid of it as soon as possible. Becoming debt free uncomplicates your life.

- **Myth 2: Pay yourself first and start saving for your retirement.** The problem with doing this is that you're getting less than 1% return in your savings account, when, instead, you could use that money and get more than 100% return right now by paying off debt, which is the fastest way to become wealthy.

- **Myth 3: Why pay off a 3% interest rate home loan when I can make 7% investing?** We must remember that we are really getting more than 100% return by paying off our principal payment on our loans. And again, who says we are going to get 7% in the market? In some years, the market has dropped by 35%.

- **Myth 4: Buy the most expensive house you can afford.** This just keeps you in debt longer and adds many more expenses to your life. The more expensive the house, the more you will pay in property taxes, home maintenance, home upgrades, yard maintenance and (if you live in such a neighborhood) community dues. You now must upgrade your lifestyle to keep up with the neighbors. Instead, buy someone *else's* dream house that fits your needs. You will save 20% versus building your own house and sidestep the headaches of construction. Dr. Doug Carlsen says that home maintenance, property taxes and upgrades average 2% of your home's value per year for a modest home. Thus, a $500K home will need $10,000 per year. Unfortunately, that peripheral cost of 2% will increase with a more expensive home. Often, you'll pay 3% for a $1.5M home and more than 4% for a $2M+ home. Yes, doctors can pay $80K or more each year for their "trophy" home. In Chapter 5, Dr. James M. Dahle, the author of *The White Coat Investor,* gives some good reasons why renting a home has its advantages during certain times in your career. Go to: https://www.whitecoatinvestor .com and type in "Should I buy or rent?"

- **Myth 5: Emergency-fund myth.** Some financial advisors recommend saving three to six months of living expenses in an emergency fund before you start paying off debt. The problem with this approach is that you never get around to paying off the debt, because it takes about two years to save up that amount. Meanwhile, many people take out the money for non-emergency items. You must begin to see debt as a tax, and automatically pay 10% to 20% of your monthly income toward the principal on your debt. Once your credit cards are paid off, you do have an emergency fund, you can get a line of credit or home-equity loan, or you can just stop paying those accelerated payments for one or two months. If you feel you need some money set aside, put $1,000 into a money market account after your credit cards are paid off using your extra found money. Once your cars are paid off, you can increase it to $5,000.

- **Myth 6: The budgeting myth.** Again, many good financial advisors recommend you observe where you're spending your money and then budget so much each month, which allows you to set aside money to pay off debts. The problem is, this gives you a false sense of security, and there is usually nothing left at the end of the month. The secret of debt elimination is to automatically take 10% to 20% out of your bank account each month to pay off debt—as if it were a tax. I can guarantee you that, if you take 10% to 20% out each month and pay it toward debt, you still will be broke at the end of the month, just like you are now, except that you will be well on your way to becoming debt free.

- **Myth 7: College-funding myth.** Many people recommend that you start funding your child's education early, so that you have enough when they're ready for school. They might recommend 529 plans that are run by different states, which have high-load, actively managed funds. The returns are dismal. You also have less control over the money. It is better to focus on debt reduction; when you're debt free, you can easily fund your children's college education with cash. Create a high cash value personal bank for each of your children to fund college. Check out chapter 8 and personalbank4u.com.

- **Myth 8: The "more money" myth.** I've heard so many people say, "If I just had more money...." When I first began my coaching program, I showed clients how to make more money, but I forgot to teach them about getting out of debt. They just got into larger amounts of debt and are now trapped in their large homes and large, high-stress lives. More money will not make you happy, but if you are focused on eliminating your debt, your life will become much less stressful.

- **Myth 9: Life insurance as an investment.** This may be true with the standard whole-life insurance policies that are regularly sold, but with a high cash value whole-life insurance policy, it could be one of your best investments. Most insurance salesmen are unaware of this type of policy. To learn more about infinite banking and how to create your own Personal Bank, check out the resources at personalbank4U.com.

- **Myth 10: Monthly payments are normal.** Our culture has taught us that we always need to be in debt. This makes a lot of money for many people in the banking and investment industries. So, stop paying them 100% interest.

- **Myth 11: Avoid-paying-taxes myth.** Many people lose money by trying different schemes to prevent paying taxes. You should want to *pay more taxes than anyone else* because it indicates you are *making more money than anyone.* Rely on your CPA. A good CPA will keep you honest and make sure you don't give more to the government than you need to.

- **Myth 12: Financial-advisor myth.** There is an old saying, "A broker will invest your money until you are broke." In the past, it was much more complicated to invest in the markets, because people had to go to different brokerage houses and work through brokers. With the Internet, it is easy to create an account online and find low-load index funds that will beat 96% of all the financial advisors because of the minimal 1% to 3% to manage your investments. Remember, a 1% advisory fee could cost you $1.5 million over twenty years if you had a $1.2 million 401(k) and you contributed $72,000 per year with an 8% return. For non-retirement money, use the free Schwab advisors, and contribute each month into the S&P 500 index fund.

- **Myth 13: Myth of bi-weekly mortgage payments.** It is true that paying your mortgage twice a month will cause a 30-year mortgage to be paid off in about twenty-two years and save 25% of the interest. This strategy creates a false sense of security and keeps you from getting totally out of debt, including paying off the home, in five to seven years and saving 80% of the interest.

- **Myth 14: Don't pay off your house early because you can write off the interest rate on your taxes.** One of the biggest misconceptions that banks and accountants perpetuate is that you should not pay off your house early because you can write off the interest on your taxes. If we look at this closely, in 2018 an average American couple who paid $10,000 a year in interest had the choice of either taking the standard deduction of $24,000 or to itemize their return and take the $10,000 tax write-off. When they itemize, they are unable to take the standard deduction of $24,000 and have an overall loss of $14,000.

Avoiding Financial Mistakes

Warren Buffett said, *"The first rule of investment is don't lose money. The second rule of investment is never forget rule number one."* The most important way to keep your wealth is never to make a big financial mistake. Big financial mistakes usually occur because of greed and ego. I have known numerous individuals who have lost their entire portfolio in a get-rich-quick scheme. Such schemes range from real estate deals to limited partnerships; they can take the form of just about anything else that sounds too good to be true. Remember, *there is no free lunch*. When you have a systematic guide to get out of debt, increase your business profitability and conservatively invest in the US market, then you will become economically free in a fairly short time. Why take a risk on anything else? If you just stick with the boring *Dr. Ace's Financial Freedom* philosophy of investing, you'll never put your retirement money at risk. Here are some other financial mistakes you should avoid.

- **Not stopping to find out what makes you happy.** The things that really make me happy are very simple and cost almost nothing. If I had known this earlier at the deepest level, I would not have needed to drive myself so hard to be successful. This is why the process of writing a new story is so important. Write down what you want your average day to look like. What are the things that make you happy? (Don't include shopping!) What are the happiest times you've enjoyed in your life? When you know who you are, it is easy to save money. Usually the simplest and least-expensive things make you happy. Try to spend the least amount of money trying to figure out what makes you happy. Rent your way through the discovery process (for example, rent that lovely condo in the mountains rather than buy it). Most people live a life of high debt and stress because they spend money, hoping it will make them happy. I guarantee that more money or things will not give you peace or happiness.

- **Allowing our ego to ruin our lives** by creating an unconscious compulsion to enhance one's identity through association with and purchase of expensive items, e.g., jewelry, exotic cars and luxury homes. Yet, rarely do these purchases satisfy the ego desires that make one feel different and special.

- **Lending money to friends and family.** If you lend money to friends or family, please realize there is a good possibility you will never be repaid. Often this has a negative impact on the relationship. If lending the money is meaningful to you, then consider simply giving it as a gift. Never co-sign a loan; in most cases, you will end up paying the loan. A co-signer is a fool with a pen.

- **Falling for get-rich-quick schemes and scams.** Never get involved in any investment that you don't completely understand. With this guide, you do not have to take risks. You already have it made. When you are asked to invest in something new, just tell them that you invest only in no-load S&P 500 or the US stock market, but thanks anyway. Check out: https://www.whitecoatinvestor. com/12-rules-to-help-you-avoid-getting-scammed/

- **Listening to investment financial advisors** who say they can beat the market. Only a fool would say they can beat the market, so just stick with no-load index funds that you can buy yourself from Schwab or Vanguard.

- **Getting into a limited partnership.** You lose control as a limited partner and are the last to be paid. Stay away from any investment or arrangement that you do not understand thoroughly or over which you do not have personal control regarding decisions.

- **Living in a high-cost, high-congestion and high-tax area.** If you choose to work and live in a large city like San Francisco or New York City, where homes can be two to three times more expensive, you will find that traffic is terrible and that there are high state and city taxes that can delay your becoming debt free and financially free. Think about moving to a tax-free state such as Texas, Florida, Wyoming, Washington, Alaska, New Hampshire, South Dakota, Tennessee or Nevada. Live in a smaller, less-expensive and safer community, and be able to buy a nicer and bigger home that you can pay off in five to seven years.

- **Buying too big a house.** Consider what you really need. Buying a bigger house than you need wastes money monthly. The cost of your home should not exceed 2.5 times your gross salary.

- **Buying a vacation home or large boat that you rarely use.** If this adds meaning to your life and you use it often, like more than sixty days a year, then it is worth the investment. That is, until it no longer adds meaning to your life—and at that time, you can sell it. It is not a bad idea for some properties like vacation homes or boats to be shared with other owners to dilute the expenses.

- **Buying timeshares.** Never buy them. You have a greater selection and a much lower price if you go to vacation rental by owner (VRBO.com).

- **Buying annuities.** Never buy them.

- **Starting another business** before you start making your own business successful. A well-run business can be very profitable. Maintain your focus, and start having fun again in your business.

- **Marry the right person the first time.** Stay away from spenders. Find someone who is conservative in their spending habits and has financial goals like yours.

- **Not getting a prenuptial agreement if you have assets.** Get your spouse (male or female) to sign on the dotted line before you say, "I do."

- **Having too many "successful" marriages.** Before divorcing, try to reinvent your relationship and work through a counselor to see if you can make the relationship work. If there is no possibility of working it out, then you both deserve your freedom. There's often a lot of anger and trying to "get even" in the divorce process. I recommend you offer your spouse a generous settlement and treat her/him with kindness and respect. Always try to maintain strong relationships with your children; never put down your partner. If your spouse wants more and does not accept your generous offer, then tell your attorney that his or her job is simply to get you in front of the judge, and no longer communicate with your spouse's attorney. This will save both of you a lot money in attorney fees. Judges are normally fair in their settlements. If you continue to marry the same type of person (alcoholic, co-dependent, crazy), then this is the time for some personal growth and counseling.

CHAPTER 5

Understand Investing and How the Markets Work

Daniel Solin has written many must-read investment books. In two of these books, *The Smartest Money Book You'll Ever Read* and *The Smartest Investment Book You'll Ever Read,* he summarized the key points about investing:

- It is not complicated.

- No one has a clue about where the market is headed.

- Stay away from individual stocks that expose you to higher risk without higher expected returns.

- Stay away from actively managed mutual funds (brokers) that increase your fees, cost, and reduce your expected return.

- Never use the services of a broker or advisor who claims to be able to beat the market.

- Determine your asset allocation and invest in low-cost index funds such as the S&P 500 (passively managed) index fund, which will beat 96% of all financial advisors and brokers. There are other, more conservative, investments listed below.

- The free-market system works. Stock prices are random and efficient. There is no mispricing. Always stay in the market.

- Don't listen to the news (turn off the noise).

Understanding the Risks of the Market

Very few people understand the stock market, and no one can accurately predict changes in the market. Jack Bogle, the founder of Vanguard group, says, *"Nobody knows nothing about the market."* Many brokers tell you to buy a stock when it is high and tell you not to buy when it drops. But common sense would tell us the best time to buy stocks is when they're low. Even worse, some brokers tell you to get out of the market when it drops. When we invest in equities (stocks), we are always on shifting sands; we are always taking a risk. And when we invest, we should not invest in actively managed mutual funds but stay with low-cost passively managed index funds such as the S&P 500, which has consistently done better than 96% of all funds on the market.

When you have a guide for obtaining financial freedom that is safe and predictable, why take a risk? Anyone who can work and save money has it made; financial freedom is yours for the taking. Your ability to earn money and pay off debt is the most important thing in developing economic abundance. Your income is like a large inflation-protected bond that allows you to put a greater amount of your investment portfolio into stocks. Investments are for added income for your retirement, not to make you rich. Your earnings from your job will make you rich if you live within your means and consistently save or store part of them. Individuals who do this now work two to three days a week and continue to do something they really enjoy that brings in money. They will never, ever use up the money they've set aside for retirement.

The Big Scam

According to *Forbes* ("Why the Average Investor's Return Is So Low," by Sean Hanlon, April 24, 2014), over a ten-year period (2004 to 2013), the S&P 500 has averaged 7.4% return. The reason average investors have realized only a

2.6% return during that same time is because they are in actively managed funds, which constantly trade in and out of the market, and the investors pay high fees in commissions, trading fees and taxes to their brokers. Many brokers buy and sell securities within the funds repeatedly, to try to improve their performance. This boosts transaction cost and taxes. These costs are buried in your management fees, which compensate the fund manager. These can cost you up to 3% to 4% annually. Many fund managers keep money in cash, so they can time the market. This is called *cash drag* and gives you a zero performance on that money, compared with what you could've gotten in an index fund.

Most individual investors rely upon money managers, advisors and brokers who engage in hyperactive trading to try to beat the market by picking winners and timing the market. This is a losing strategy. In most cases, investors would be better off consistently investing in index funds like the S&P 500. Jack Bogle, founder of the Vanguard group, believes in index funds and says actively managed funds are a big scam. When you invest in loaded, actively managed mutual funds, you put up 100% of the capital and take 100% of the risk, and if you make money, they take up to 70% or more of the upside in fees. And if you lose money, they still get paid. They are charging you 10 to 30 times what it would cost for you to buy a low-cost index fund that would match the market and beat 96% of the mutual funds. Because fees are the enemy of the individual investor, we need to stay away from financial advisors and brokers who work on commission and thus put us into actively managed funds.

Here is an example from one of my clients who had more than $1.6 million that was managed by a large brokerage firm. Over a six-year period, his portfolio would have built *$863,881 more in assets* if it had been placed into a Schwab S&P 500 fund. Compare your portfolio to the S&P 500, and see how you do. Go to Doctorace.com for more videos and audios, and download and fill out the Excel comparison sheet seen below.

Remember, the S&P 500 fund performs better than 96% of all other managed funds, and I have yet to see any of my clients whose portfolio has done better than the S&P 500 index fund. In most cases, they have lost significant amounts of money when they let the experts invest for them.

	Schwab S&P 500 mutual fund index annual return	Brokerage **trust** account	annual % return	**Loss**	Brokerage **401K** account	annual % return	**Loss**
Ticker sym	SWPPX						
Fees	0.03%		1%				
Cost/ 1M$	$300		$10,000				
Stocks/Bonds	100%/0		100%/0				
Invested		Opening balance			Opening balance		
2017	21.80%	$406,560	12.00%	($39,843)	$1,276,633	9.50%	($157,026)
2016	12.0%	$321,784	6.5%	($17,698)	$1,099,332	1.27%	($117,958)
2015	1.4%	$316,367	−2.3%	($11,706)	$1,262,352	−2.28%	($46,455)
2014	13.7%	$302,687	4.5%	($27,847)	$1,322,966	6.29%	($98,032)
2013	32.4%	$356,161	7.9%	($87,259)	$1,186,118	11.37%	($249,441)
2012	16.0%	$272,222	12.1%	($10,617)		Loss	**($668,911)**
			Loss	**($194,970)**			
						Total Loss	**($863,881)**

	Schwab S&P 500 mutual fund index	Brokerage **taxable** account Opening balance each year	Added money that year	total invested	Your brokerage return that year	Loss (red) Gain (black)
Ticker sym	SWPPX					
Fees	0.03%					
Cost/ 1M$	$300			1%		
Stocks/Bonds	100%/0			$10,000		
Invested		Opening balance	Added Money	100%/0		
2018	−4.40%			$0		
2017	21.80%			$0		
2016	12.0%			$0		

	Schwab S&P 500 mutual fund index	Brokerage **taxable** account Opening balance each year	Added money that year	total invested	Your brokerage return that year	Loss (red) Gain (black)
2015	1.4%			$0		
2014	13.7%			$0		
2013	32.4%			$0		
2012	16.0%			$0		
2011	2.1%			$0		
2010	15%			$0		
2009	26.30%			$0		
					Total Loss/gain	

Another must-read book is Anthony Robbins' *Unshakeable*. He writes about the two enemies of the investor: fear and fees. Most money is lost in the market because of these two factors. If you are an investor and put your money in an actively managed mutual fund, you will pay 3.17% of the non-taxable account toward fees (4.17% if it's a taxable account). Look at the chart below to see what this 3% difference in fees would cost you over 20, 30, or 40 years if the S&P 500 average 7% growth. You would have two to three times more earnings.

	4% growth	7% growth	Earnings difference
20 Years	$191,996	$425,948	2.2X
30 years	$504,544	$1,300,631	2.6X
40 years	$1,058,851	$3,220,187	3.1X

The second-greatest enemy of the investor is fear. Getting out of the market when it starts to drop is a mistake. This is the time you need to *buy*. You have a good portfolio of index funds you should always stay in, because they will always rebound. From 1997 to 2016, the S&P 500 index returned 7.7%. If you were out of the market during the top ten days, your return would've dropped to 4%; the top 20 days, your return would've been 1.6%;

and if you were out of the market the top 40 days, your return would've been a *negative* 2.4%. The message is clear: when the market drops, *do not* get out of the market, and continually keep buying more index funds like the S&P 500 as it drops. The free-market system works. Stock prices are random and efficient. There is no mispricing. Always stay in the market.

Understanding Index Funds

Many *individual* stocks are not safe on a long-term basis, which is why we focus on *index funds* that represent the whole United States market and thus spread the risk across many securities. Warren Buffett, the legendary investor and business magnate, believes in the American economy and has said that he would invest the money he leaves to his children in a Vanguard S&P 500 fund. An index fund is a passively managed mutual fund made up of the securities (stocks or bonds) in a stock index in the proportions the index devises. The most followed stock-market indexes are the Dow Jones industrial average (DJIA) and the Standard and Poor's 500 (S&P 500). The DJIA is based on 30 major companies; the S&P 500 has 500 companies; the NASDAQ has 3900 listings, and the Wilshire 5000 total market index is the broadest index for the US stock market.

The advantages of investing in index funds are as follows:

• Passive investing (avoids excessive fees, commissions and taxes)

• Diversification spreads risk across many securities

• Low management fees

• Income from dividend returns

• Predictable risk (lower than individual securities)

• Easy to purchase by yourself without paying brokerage fees

• Performance better than 96% of actively managed funds

Actively Managed Funds Compared to Index (Passively Managed) Funds

In actively managed funds, the financial advisor or broker tries to beat the market by timing the market and selecting winning stocks. This results in the client's money moving into and out of the market numerous times and leads to a high commission for the financial advisor and expenses to the investor through trading costs, short-term capital gains tax and cash drag (money held out of the market and not being invested). These expenses significantly reduce your overall return, and most of these funds never beat the average S&P 500 index fund. This 3% to 4% (400 basis points) expense results in a 50% to 70% loss in the return of your investments over time. This is why fees are so important. You can get an S&P 500 index fund for as little as 0.03% (3 basis points), which mirrors the components of a market index and has no other costs.

Corrections in the Market

There are always corrections in the market, and you must welcome them as a great opportunity to buy more index funds on sale. This is a paradigm shift, and we must develop an attitude of excitement, not fear, when the market drops, because that's when stocks are on sale. Below is a chart of the average historical corrections of the market from 1900 to 2015.

Average Historical Corrections of the Market				
	Regular Decline (5% or more)	Modest Correction (10% or more)	Serious Correction (15% or more)	Bear Market (20% or more)
Frequency	3 times/year	1 time/year	Every 2 years	Every 3 years
Average loss before drop ends	11%	19%	27%	35%
Average duration	40 days	109 days	217 days	364 days

In his recent book *Unshakeable*, Tony Robbins states that, over the past 70 years, there have been only 14 bear markets, averaging one every five years, lasting an average of one year and ranging from 45 days to nearly two years. He says that what you need to know is that bear markets don't last and are always followed by a bull market during the next 12 months. From March 9, 2009, the S&P 500 index surged by 69.5% over the next 12 months.

Since 2009, we have not had a bear market (20% or more drop) and only one 17% drop in 2010 and an 18% drop in 2011. Since then, we have had only 10 corrections in the S&P 500 that were greater than 10%. 2018 was a very volatile year, with drops of 7%, 11% and 19.7%. This is probably because of the ending of the Federal Reserve's policy of quantitative easing from 2009 to 2014 and low interest rates, forcing more investors into the market. 2018 was a great year to test your risk tolerance and an excellent year to buy stocks at the bottom. Even though there were significant corrections, the overall loss that year was a –4.4%. Remember, it becomes a loss only if you sell.

Your Personal Bank and the stock market is just a place to store your money for better long-term returns for retirement. Long-term investing in Index funds like the S&P 500 can give you 3 to 4 times the return, compared to a less-risky bond portfolio. When you are debt free, it becomes easier to invest into stocks like the S&P 500. For most investors, this is all we need to do, and we can quit worrying about the market.

Dealing with Your Investment Emotions

As humans, we are wired with a fight-or-flight emotional base. Our emotions make life worth living, but uncontrolled emotions while investing can be deadly. I highly recommend that you read Jason Zweig's book entitled *Your Money and Your Brain: How the New Science of Neuroeconomics Can Help Make You Rich*. It will help you understand your emotions during investing. If you are unable to understand or cannot discipline and control your emotions when there is a 10%, 20% or even 40% drop in the market, then you should place your money in your Personal Bank and not worry about the market. Great investors spend little time watching the market but do have a simple and safe game plan that they stick with. They have patience, available cash and courage, and they know market history well enough to wait for the drops in the market that always come. Once you understand the history of the market, then you respond with logic instead of a knee-jerk reaction from your fear. Stop listening to the financial (all) news throughout the year. Some investors continue to contribute monthly, automatically, to the S&P 500 or US total stock market index fund in your Schwab account through dollar-cost averaging (DCA). Others put their money in their Personal Bank and money market account, wait for a greater-than 10% drop in the market, and buy more, using their discretionary income if the market drops further. That's it, you're done. Remember: Being debt free and having a paid-off home and business, cash value in a Personal Bank and a steady income puts 90% of your net worth in inflation-adjusted, secure bond-like assets. This allows the 10% to 20% of your net worth to be invested in equities such as the S&P 500 without worry, knowing you are in it for the long game. It is that simple.

What Do You Do When the Market Tanks?

When the stock market drops and we see our portfolio being reduced, our fight-or-flight emotions are stimulated. Long-term investors get excited rather than depressed because they realize the opportunities they have been given by this drop. Below is a step-by-step approach for you to remember during downturns in the market.

1. Understand and control your emotions. You need to switch your emotions to excitement because you are now able to use your built-up cash in your money-market account to buy the S&P 500 or dividend-paying stocks *on sale*. Warren Buffett says that opportunities of a 15% to 30% bear-market drop rarely occur, and when they do, you need to buy as much of the good companies or S&P 500 as you can while they are on sale.

2. Remember that you have seen this picture before and you know how it ends, so **never sell, only buy** when the market drops.

3. Warren Buffett said if you can detach yourself from the crowd and become greedy while others are fearful, you can become very rich, and you don't have to be smart. It does not take brains; it takes temperament.

4. Remind yourself that you are debt free, that you have a constant source of income and that these great opportunities occur only a few times in your life.

5. Start rounding up more cash and hope it drops further for even greater opportunities.

6. Wonder what Warren Buffett is thinking (he is very happy).

7.   Get back to loving your life.

Stop listening to all the financial advice on television. This is just noise. Once you are debt free and have a highly profitable, effortless and fun business, you never have to worry about money again. Saving money in your Personal Bank and investing in index fund when there are drops in the market is the most efficient way to save your money and become rich slowly. You do not care about the market. Warren Buffett said if the stock market closed down for five years, it would not make a difference in his decision to invest. Remember to always stay in the market, and understand that drops in the market are opportunities to buy.

Steps to Individual Investing on Your Own

When you learn to invest on your own, you become the chess player instead of the chess piece. With the internet, investing in the market on your own is very simple. You first need to open a brokerage account with a well-known investment company that provides excellent service with low fees and a wide range of low-cost index funds. I believe that both Vanguard and Schwab are excellent companies. **So, do it** today. I have accounts with both Vanguard and Schwab, but I find that Schwab is more customer oriented. It is open 24 hours a day, seven days a week and has excellent representatives and brokers. Schwab also requires no dollar minimums to open an account, the lowest expense ratios, and when you buy its mutual funds and index ETFs (exchange-traded funds), there are no trading costs, compared to other companies. All other trades are only $4.95 a trade.

All representatives and brokers from Schwab and Vanguard are salaried; they do not work on commission, so their advice focuses on your best interests. The company also has agents located in most cities. These local Schwab brokers can help you through the process, or you may go online and have an account set up within 30 minutes. Because you are transferring your accounts to them, ask to get 20 free trades. Once you set up an account, then you can start putting money into specific mutual funds or follow some of the strategies that I will mention below. I also recommend becoming familiar with the Yahoo Finance and Morningstar websites to help you best understand the past performance of different funds.

Investment Strategies

If you follow this guide, get out of debt and make more money, you will never have to worry about money. Most individuals could be totally debt free in seven to ten years. Just don't do stupid things with money. Now, stop worrying. In chapter 6 are investment options to put your mind at ease, knowing you are getting the best return on your investments within your risk tolerance without paying high fees and commissions. Pick the options that work best for you and your risk tolerance, and then you're done. It's that simple.

The best investment strategies are always simple and easy to understand. Brokers want to sell you complex investments that you don't understand so they can charge high fees and commissions, which often results in lower returns to you as the investor. Once you understand your risk tolerance and how the market works over time, then select the options that fit your comfort zone and your desired rate of return. Remind yourself that you are a long-term investor, and then stay in the market during corrections. When the market drops, you should be elated because stocks are on sale, and this is the time to buy and add to your portfolio. But before you invest, you should first understand your asset allocation and risk tolerance.

Investment Strategies Need to Change with the Times

The way we invest today is dramatically different than it was forty years ago. We can now go online, open a brokerage account with Schwab or Vanguard, and buy low-cost index funds that match the market and do better than 96% of all actively managed funds. In 1980, mortgage interest rates reached an all-time high of 18.4%, and you could buy a 14%, non-callable, 30-year, AAA-rated, tax-free municipal bond. That was when you would buy only bonds. In early 2000, you could buy 10-year, AAA-rated, tax-free municipal bonds at 5% or 6% with a guaranteed after-tax yield of 8% to 9%. Back then, there was no need to risk your money in the stock market.

Over the past 15 years, interest rates have decreased to almost 0%. A 10-year treasury note or CD is getting only about a 2.5% return, and this does not even keep up with inflation. This is a tragedy for those who are retired, living on a fixed income, and relying on the interest from their investments. Fifteen years ago, they were getting around a 5% return in their bank saving accounts, and now they are getting less than 1%. If you are relying upon the interest from bonds to live on in your retirement, you may run out of money and may have to add more stock index funds to your portfolio.

The more averse you are to risk, the more of your portfolio should be in in your Personal Bank with an average tax-free return of around 5%, which is like a before-tax return of around 8% to 9%. When you are buying stock index funds such as the S&P 500 and the total US stock index fund, you are buying United States businesses that, over time, will return three to four times what bond funds will earn. Many of these US businesses do have international holdings. You must see stock index funds investments as a savings account and stay in for the long term. Stock index funds are less risky the longer you hold them, while the longer the maturity of bonds, the riskier they become. But if you are one who gets upset with price fluctuations in the stock market, then you should not own stocks. Put more of your money into your Personal Bank and any extra into high-yielding bank CDs, Schwab money market accounts or short-term two- to five-year US treasury bonds.

Remember, even if we get a 10% return with our stock (S&P 500) portfolio, your real return would be about 7% once adjusted to 3% inflation. A portfolio of 50% stocks and 50% bonds has an expected return of only 6%, and, after adjusting for inflation of 3%, you are now down to a return of 3%. That is why we need to eliminate the 1% fee you pay your advisor and the 2% fee for the mutual fund, which could leave us with 0% return. If you invested in bonds returning only about 2%, you would have a negative return. Because of the current historical low interest rates, bonds return only about 2%.

Remember your history

Warren Buffett likes to quote Mark Twain when he supposedly said, "History doesn't repeat itself, but it often rhymes." Michael Alexander wrote a book entitled *Stock Cycles*. He reviews the markets over 200 years of American history until the year 2000. During that time, we have had seven long-term bear and seven long-term bull markets. The total average real return in a long-term bull market was 13.2%, while the average return in a long-term bear market was 0.3%. For example, from 1966 to 1982, the total real return was a –1.5%. But from 1982 to 2000, the average total real return of the market was 14.8%. Alexander then went on to predict that, starting in 2000, there would be a long-term bear market. In March 2013, the price of the Standard & Poor's (S&P) 500 was 1527, the same price as it was in March 2000, resulting in no growth of the stock, which is why those 13 years are called "the lost decade." Also, that time period was a very turbulent time for investors, but an exceptionally great time for those understood the phrase by Warren Buffett, who once said that as an investor, it is wise to *"be fearful when others are greedy and greedy when others are fearful."* Today many investors think the market is reaching its peak, which may be one reason why Warren Buffett, as of January 2019, has more than $111 billion in cash equivalents. It has been more than 10 years since we have had a bear market, and, like Warren, I am keeping a majority of my powder dry. After funding my Personal Bank, I will automatically put money into my Schwab account monthly, keeping more money in liquid assets such as US treasuries and money-market accounts that are returning more than 2%. The cash value in my Personal Bank and the liquid assets in my treasury and money-market accounts will allow me to take advantage of possible opportunities if the market drops 10% to 35% over the next one to three years. Remember, no one can predict the market, so, on this matter, you must make your own decision.

CHAPTER 6

The Best Investment Options

Option 1a: Pay off all debt. Safe! No Risk! Highest Tax-Free Return!!!

Paying off debt is mandatory *before* investing and is like getting the highest-grade inflation-protected bond with a guaranteed interest rate of more than 100%, risk-free. Set up an automatic payment each month toward the principal of your next debt in your debt-elimination payments.

Option 1b: Create Your Own Personal Bank. Safe! No Risk! Tax-Free Return!

Creating your own Personal Bank comes from the concept of infinite banking by Nelson Nash in the 1980s. It has also been known as Private Family Bank, Bank on Yourself, Infinite Banking or High Cash Value Life Insurance. It uses a specially designed high cash value whole life insurance policy that maximizes cash value in the policy enabling you to store your money safely while receiving a tax-free guaranteed 4% to 5% return. Plus, it provides a death benefit for your family. Like a savings account, the cash value in the policy can be used and accessed at any time for any reason. This option is for everyone but especially for those who are fearful of the risks and the volatility of the stock market. The main purpose of your own Personal Bank is to provide a place to save money while receiving a high tax-free yield, build wealth and create a consistent stream of income to invest and to use for retirement. When debt free, you need a place to keep your wealth tax free and never have to borrow from a bank again because now you can borrow from your own Personal Bank.

Creating your own Personal Bank would entail working with a life insurance agent who meets specific criteria. This agent must know how to design a whole life insurance policy that maximizes cash value and satisfies the IRS's non-MEC requirements. They should also work with the top four mutual insurance companies, which are Mass Mutual, Guardian, New York Life, and Northwestern mutual. These 4 major mutual companies all have a guaranteed rate of 4% and pay a surplus in addition. The guaranteed rate plus the surplus equates to the total dividend rate. The top 4 companies paid rates between 5.00%–6.40% for 2019. These companies have always paid a dividend for the 160+ years they've been around. Lafayette Life insurance company is another highly rated mutual company that is used by many agents who provide high cash value whole life insurance policies. If you work with these agents, make sure that the policy is designed so no more than 10% of premiums go to the base death benefit and the rest is directed toward cash value.

These are "mutually owned" life insurance companies that enable you to participate in the company's profits and dividends at the end of the year. Correctly designed policies maximize your cash accumulation by putting 10% of your premium toward death benefits and 90% toward cash value and small term rider. This reduces an agent's commission by 70% to 90%. The policy's primary use is to hold and build cash in a guaranteed tax-deferred 4% to 5% return safe environment to be used for future investments with the death benefit being secondary. The life insurance policy gives you more safety, liquidity, flexibility and control of your money than any savings vehicle or retirement plan you will own. This is why it has been used by major banks, Fortune 500 Companies, and the wealthy for more than a century and is often their # 1 Asset.

The cash value in the policy grows tax free and all money borrowed from the policy is tax-free. You earn a guaranteed tax free 4% to 5% each year including dividends. This is what the average stock investor earns each year except the returns from your Personal Bank are tax free. Within the first year, more than 85% of the premiums are now available as cash value. On average, after 3 to 4 years all your premiums paid are available in cash value. Money can be retrieved from your account for any reason through a loan process without any application or approval by using your cash value as collateral. You borrow from the company's general fund at a 5% interest rate. Because you borrow the money from the insurance company's general fund all cash value in your policy continues to grow at around 5%, which is as good as a free loan.

As an example, if you have $100,000 in cash value, you can borrow up to $100,000 from the company's general fund using your cash value as collateral. This leaves your cash value intact to continue to earn your guaranteed 5% return on the $100,000. Over the next 10 years you will have paid $27,268 in loan interest back to the insurance company. During that same 10 years your $100,000 in your cash value has earned $64,701 in interest and dividends! In fact, the growth of your cash value has covered the $27,268 of loan interest and has given you a $37,433 profit. Even though the 5% interest is the same on the growth and the loan, you are always earning the 5% interest and dividends on an ever-increasing cash value balance while the 5% you are paying on the loan is on a decreasing loan balance. Because you are borrowing the money and not withdrawing the money from your cash value, there are no taxes on the capital gains. During your retirement years, you can borrow money each year from your cash value tax-free and never pay it back. The interest and money you borrowed will be deducted from your death benefits.

When borrowing money from your policy, understand that there is a difference between non-direct recognition and direct recognition insurance companies. When you borrow from a non-direct recognition company, they do not recognize that you borrowed money from your cash value and will continue to credit you the same dividends and interest as if you never took out a loan. The loan interest on the borrowed money goes to the insurance company. The death benefit and cash value will be reduced by the loan payment until the loan is paid back. You will still earn their yearly dividend rate on the total cash value and when the loan is paid back, the death benefits and cash value are completely restored as if you never had a loan. Mass Mutual insurance is an example of a non-direct recognition company.

With a direct recognition company such as Guardian, you will receive their dividend rate on all money still in cash value. You will also receive a slightly different dividend on the money that is outstanding in policy loans, which closely matches whatever the loan interest rate. With some direct recognition insurance companies, the dividend paid on the loan portion can be significantly lower than your loan interest rate. This is usually true with smaller companies, so always check with the agent to determine the historical dividend paid on borrowed money. The main take away is that direct recognition companies still pay a dividend on borrowed money but at different rates. Guardian insurance company is a direct recognition company and currently pays a slightly higher dividend on borrowed money. Guardian also has an option to change your policy from a direct recognition to a non-direct recognition at year 10.

The question is how much do you want to save? This is a high-powered savings program with a death benefit. You must see the premiums not as bills but deposits into your cash value savings account. So how big do you want your cash value (savings) to grow over time? The cash value is a combination of the premiums you pay and the interest and dividends that the policy earns each year. This creates an exponential growth curve.

Most life insurance policies are sold on how cheaply they can provide a death benefit. They say that you should buy term insurance and invest the difference. The problem is very few people invest the difference and less than 2% of term policies claims are paid which means all that money put into term insurance is lost. With a high cash value whole life insurance policy we want to know how much premium we can put into the policy's cash value rather than into death benefit costs. The death benefit is a bonus. The policy is designed to optimize cash value accumulation and then we will determine how much death benefit we will buy.

Because the policy is designed to increase the cash value, they add a paid-up addition (PUA) rider which provides small amounts of death benefits through term insurance that enable them to significantly increase the cash value in a much higher ratio than the base policy can. The PUA rider allows for a large cash value in your policy. The insurance companies require that at least 10% of the premiums go into life insurance (death benefit). So, 10% of your premiums go to base whole life policy and 90% goes to PUA's for cash value and a small term policy rider while making up 100% of your Personal Bank premium. Remember that the cash value grows tax free and can be accessed tax-free. That is why the tax-free 5% you are getting from your whole life insurance policy is like an 8% return in the market where you must pay capital gains taxes on your non-IRA accounts or personal income tax on withdrawals from your 401(k) plan. The comparable return may even be 9% to 10% in your Personal Bank when you consider the 2% to 4% loss in advisory or mutual fund fees and the money lost buying term insurance.

In designing the plan, your agent must be knowledgeable about how much cash is built into the policy to ensure the policy is not classified as a modified endowment contract (MEC) based on the IRS Seven Pay rule. In 1988 the tax law changed because certain insurance policies funded cash value too rapidly and were classified as a modified endowment contract. The IRS eliminated the use of such policies as short-term tax-free savings vehicles by imposing stiff penalties. The IRS created the Seven Pay Test rule were the IRS limits the total amount you can pay into a policy in any consecutive seven years of its existence. This amount is compared to the sum of the net level premiums that could have been paid on a guaranteed seven-year pay whole life policy providing the same death benefits. If you tried to put too many premium dollars in the cash value compared to the policy's death benefit you have crossed the dreaded MEC line. To satisfy the MEC rule the death benefit is raised through a cheap term insurance rider allowing greater cash value in the policy.

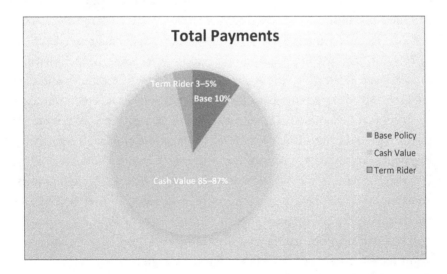

Each policy needs to be custom designed to meet each person's individual long-term financial goals, your current financial needs, your current cash flow, your current savings, and your legacy needs.

You can also borrow money for your retirement out of these policies and not pay back the loans. The Personal Bank is more like a defined benefit plan, most often known as a pension, because it promises you a set payout when you retire. Because of costs, most employers have eliminated defined benefit plans and replaced them with defined contribution plans, like a 401(k) or 403(b). These plans place the burden of investing on the employee with no guarantee of investment returns or specific benefits when they retire. Your Personal Bank has many more advantages over a regular 401(k) plan. There are no restrictions like you find in qualified retirement plans such as minimum distributions, restrictions and penalties on withdrawal before age 59, and all distributions are taxed at your personal tax rate. Your Personal Bank also allows you to make larger contributions than most traditional qualified plans. Your investment growth is tax deferred; you can access your funds tax free, and you have a death benefit with all inheritance income going tax free to your heirs.

The Personal Bank becomes your legacy and you can create participating whole life policies on yourself, your children and your grandchildren and be the owner of each policy. As these children get older, the policies' cash value can be used to buy their first car, help with their college education, weddings and their new business. The children re-pay these loans back to your bank.

The Personal Bank is the ideal saving vehicle for your children's education. In contrast, if your child needs to take out a private loan, they will have to fill out a loan application. The application has all the income and credit score requirements of any regular bank loan. If the student has no credit history, a co-signer may be required. The student or co-signer's FICO score determines the loan's interest rate. The co-signer is obligated for the loan's repayment. Repayment consistency affects the co-signer's FICO score. Compare this to a Personal Bank student loan application where there is no application process. You simply submit the loan amount to the insurance company and receive the money in about 5 business days.

Comparing a normal student loan repayment plan, the student must begin repaying most federal student loans right after s/he leave college or drop below half-time enrollment, plus loans start repayment once the loan is fully disbursed (paid out). That can even be while the student is still in school. A Personal Bank student loan, on the other hand, can be paid back however and whenever you, the policy owner, choose.

Let's compare a 529 plan to using a Personal Bank. Withdrawals from a 529 plan are tax-free to the extent your child (or other account beneficiary) incurs Qualified Higher Education Expenses (QHEE) during the year. If you withdraw more than the QHEE, the excess is a non-qualified distribution. Whoever receives this non- qualified money will have to report taxable income and pay a 10% federal penalty tax on the earnings portion of the non-qualified distribution. You CANNOT include the following expenses: insurance, sports or club activity fees, and many other types of fees that may be charged to your students but are not required as a condition of enrollment. The expenses for a computer may not be included unless the institution requires that students have their own computers. Other costs that may not be included are transportation costs (like bringing junior home for the holidays), repayment of student loans and room and board costs in excess of the amount the school includes in its "cost of attendance" figures for federal financial aid purposes.

529 plan Contributions cannot exceed the amount necessary to provide for the qualified education expenses of the beneficiary. Be aware that there may be gift tax consequences if your contributions, plus any other gifts, to a particular beneficiary exceed $14,000 during the year. A 529 account owned by a parent for a dependent student is reported on the federal financial aid application (FAFSA) as a parental asset. Any money remaining in a 529 account after education expenses are withdrawn is subject to standard qualified plan withdrawal and taxation rules. And, lest we forget, 529 plans are invested in mutual funds in the stock and bond markets where values fluctuate and could be down when needed.

When the Personal Bank is used for education expenses, the policy owner alone decides what the money can be used for. There is no such thing as a non-qualified distribution. There are no penalties under any circumstances. There are no regulatory limits on, or tax consequences to, how much you put into a Personal Bank for funding a child's education. While it's true that, once a policy is underwritten, it is limited to that maximum funding level. However, you can start additional policies to add any amount you want to your savings. Money saved in a Personal Bank is not reported on applications for college financial aid. Money remaining in a Personal Bank policy after education expenses have been withdrawn, grows tax-free, can be taken out tax-free, and will pass on to the beneficiary tax-free.

Ownership of the policy can also be transferred to the student. Policy cash value always goes up, so there's no fear of market volatility when the money is needed. It's much simpler, more flexible, and less risky to pay for a child's or grandchild's education through a Personal Bank policy loan than through any typical student loan. Plus, it offers a powerful additional benefit that no student loan offers, which is the death benefit on the life of the person paying into the policy. The student can be designated as the beneficiary. A trust can be designated to control responsible use of the money. The main point here is, if you live and can fully fund the Personal Bank to pay for the child's education, it's paid for. If you die before you're able to save up enough, the death benefit will fund the child's education. This is better than any other savings plan.

It can get even better. Once the student's education is complete and they have a job, the policy owner can make them a life-changing offer. If the child makes loan payments and pays off the policy loan balance over time, the parent or grandparent can agree to transfer policy ownership to the child at that time. This will not only transfer control of the policy's cash value to the child, but teaches them the value of saving, the importance of getting out of debt, conservative safe investing, and help them implement a forced savings plan for their retirement. It provides them with a wealth-building system they can continue to profit from throughout their life. Even after this transfer, let's not forget that the death benefit is still active on the parent's or grandparent's life if the child continues making at least minimum premium payments. When the insured person eventually dies, the child will receive the death benefit with instructions how to use it to start Personal Banks for their children. This can provide an opportunity to start a generational wealth-building system that will make each generation potentially wealthier than its predecessors. You can create a financial independence legacy for your family using your Personal Bank.

This is a permanent whole life policy where your annual premiums never increase. In term life and universal life insurance policies the annual premiums increase as you get older and eventually the cost of the premiums become unsustainable. Because this is a high cash value policy you can choose to stop your premium payments after just a few years allowing your premiums to be paid by the increasing growth of cash value from your guaranteed returns and dividends. If you do so you will miss out on all that tax-deferred growth and tax-free income that you would have had by continuing to fund your policy.

One of the main purposes of your Personal Bank is to pay off your debts. Every dollar you use to eliminate your debts remains in your bank, accumulating interest and dividends even when you borrow from the policy to pay off debts. The cash value in the policy acts also as an emergency fund. At the end of the process, your debts are paid off, and all the dollars you used to do it with are still in your bank, continually growing. This is also the one of the best options to transfer wealth and create a legacy for your children or grandchildren. The Personal Bank should be maximized before investing in the market because it has the following advantages:

- It is one of the safest investments, where all growth is tax free and guaranteed.

- The Personal Bank provides a tax-free vehicle to safely put the excess money that becomes available when you become debt free which is significantly higher than the limits that can be put on a retirement plan.

- Tax-free removes the uncertainty of what increase taxes could do to your retirement plan savings when you need the money the most and are the most vulnerable because you are not working.

- At the time of this writing, it has a guaranteed 4+% tax-deferred rate of return and a guaranteed locked in 5% loan rate.

- Many big-name advisors recommend you buy term insurance and invest the difference. However, many individuals don't invest the difference but spend it. The Personal Bank has built in self-discipline, ensuring you do have money in retirement.

- You may also have access to the life insurance benefits before you pass away should you have a terminal illness, critical illness or chronic illness making the policy like a long-term care policy.

- You never have to worry about the volatility of the stock market.

- You have guaranteed insurability for your life and when you die, the death benefit goes 100% tax-free to your heirs.

- You have access to the cash value in the policy without penalties or restrictions.

- You reverse the flow of interest you are paying to the bank back to paying the interest to yourself.

- You pay no income and capital-gains taxes on policy loans and most withdrawals.

- It does not require any dramatic lifestyle changes and provides money for purchases and retirement needs.

- The interest and dividends are paid on all the money you have put into the policy, even if you have borrowed money from the policy to spend.

- The owner and the insured do not have to be the same person. The wife can be the owner of the policy and the insured could be her husband or child. If sole owner, she has complete control of the cash value in the policy and not the insured. If health and age do not allow you to get the insurance you need, you own the insurance policy on the life of another person.

- The death benefit is a great side benefit to these policies. It can be critical to leave a legacy and to care for your family and can be a jump start of future wealth for your family. As the cash value grows your death benefit also grows. The older you get, the more money is passed on to your family.

- You have unrestricted liquidity, control and use of your money for any reason.

- There is great flexibility in the policy. Many people mistakenly think that you must pay premiums each year into a whole life policy to keep it active. This is just not true. You can frontload your policy with high premium payments for 2 to 4 years and then the policy is paid in full You can also reduce the amount you pay into the policy each year if you have restricted cash flow, just pay the basic premium. When you have more money, put more in. There is great flexibility and a good insurance agent can help you with your questions.

- In many states, these assets are protected from creditors, judgments and lawsuits.

- You can build your wealth tax free and access your wealth tax free (provided a MEC does not occur or a lapse or surrender with a gain as this would result in a taxable event).

- It helps you pay off debt, invest, and save at the same time. Pay off your cars, home, student loans and credit cards while simultaneously building retirement wealth using the same dollars.

Here is an example of a high cash value whole life policy for a 40-year-old female non-smoker with annual premiums of $10,000. Note that the cash value always continues to grow as well as the death benefit. At age 65 her cash value has grown to $445,154 with a death benefit of $882,514. If she started at age 30, and put in $30,000 for 25 years, her cash value would be over $2,166,549 and have a death benefit of well over $3 million at age 65. If we use the example family in this book, who after paying off their debt, will have over $30,000 annually to put toward their Personal Bank. By age 65 they would have over $1,333,462 in cash value and a death benefit of over $2.6 million. Remember, they always have available that additional $30,000 each year in their cash value to buy cars, take vacations and send their children to college while the cash value in their policy is always growing. When you become debt free, you could easily put much more into your Personal Bank such as $20,000, $30,000 or even $100,000 a year depending on your income. You will never worry about what the stock market is doing knowing that your financial and retirement needs have been guaranteed and you will be leaving a legacy for your family. Note that there is a guaranteed portion which you can always count on and the current assumption based on recent dividends which you most likely would receive.

40 YEAR OLD MALE. MASS MUTUAL POLICY. $10,000/YR – 25 YEARS						
Age/Funding			GUARANTEED		CURRENT ASSUMPTIONS	
Yr	Age	Annual Outlay	Cum. Outlay	Cash Value	Death Benefit	Cash Value	Death Benefit
1	41	$10,000	$10,000	$8,463	$277,680	$8,609	$277,680
2	42	$10,000	$20,000	$16,970	$304,425	$17,653	$304,903
3	43	$10,000	$30,000	$26,449	$330,269	$27,929	$331,688
4	44	$10,000	$40,000	$36,350	$355,250	$38,866	$358,072
5	45	$10,000	$50,000	$46,533	$379,402	$50,360	$384,093
6	46	$10,000	$60,000	$56,999	$402,760	$62,418	$409,804
7	47	$10,000	$70,000	$67,758	$425,357	$75,063	$435,241
8	48	$10,000	$80,000	$78,814	$447,226	$88,325	$460,441
9	49	$10,000	$90,000	$90,216	$468,393	$102,235	$485,444
10	50	$10,000	$100,000	$101,966	$488,883	$116,822	$510,203
11	51	$10,000	$110,000	$114,064	$508,718	$132,137	$534,736
12	52	$10,000	$120,000	$126,490	$527,921	$148,190	$559,131
13	53	$10,000	$130,000	$139,218	$546,515	$165,026	$583,397
14	54	$10,000	$140,000	$152,234	$564,526	$182,668	$607,610
15	55	$10,000	$150,000	$165,503	$581,977	$201,164	$631,795
16	56	$10,000	$160,000	$178,896	$598,895	$220,559	$656,056
17	57	$10,000	$170,000	$192,499	$615,304	$240,979	$680,456
18	58	$10,000	$180,000	$206,291	$631,227	$262,450	$705,000
19	59	$10,000	$190,000	$220,346	$646,686	$285,021	$729,699
20	60	$10,000	$200,000	$234,632	$661,700	$308,752	$754,461
21	61	$10,000	$210,000	$249,103	$676,284	$333,614	$779,344
22	62	$10,000	$220,000	$263,673	$690,457	$359,637	$804,482
23	63	$10,000	$230,000	$278,250	$704,238	$386,889	$829,973
24	64	$10,000	$240,000	$292,769	$717,647	$415,385	$855,976
25	65	$10,000	$250,000	$307,217	$730,702	$445,154	$882,514
26	66	$0		$315,137	$563,277	$467,580	$835,756
30	70	$0		$347,440	$563,277	$568,407	$921,512
35	75	$0		$388,537	$563,277	$722,183	$1,046,976
40	80	$0		$427,978	$563,277	$909,880	$1,197,526
45	85	$0		$462,366	$563,277	$1,132,824	$1,380,062
50	90	$0		$489,882	$563,277	$1,386,201	$1,593,884

Below are two charts that show a 50-year-old male, non-smoker funding $20,000 a year for just five years. After five years he will have $104,887 in cash value and $400,000 in death benefit. At age 65 he will have $141,251 in cash value. If he puts in premiums for 10 years (second chart below), at year 10 he will have $239,968 in cash value and $600,000 in death benefit. At age 65 he will have $324,905 in cash value. In both policies, the life insurance is paid up for the rest of his life and the cash value will continue to grow. As you can see there is great flexibility in these policies and in payment options.

50 YEAR OLD MALE. GUARDIAN POLICY. $20,000/YR - 5 YEARS						
Age/Funding			GUARANTEED		CURRENT ASSUMPTIONS	
Yr	Age	Annual Outlay	Cum. Outlay	Cash Value	Death Benefit	Cash Value	Death Benefit
1	50	$20,000	$20,000	$17,619	$400,000	$17,619	$400,000
2	51	$20,000	$40,000	$37,065	$400,000	$37,854	$400,000
3	52	$20,000	$60,000	$56,691	$400,000	$58,664	$400,000
4	53	$20,000	$80,000	$77,061	$400,000	$81,139	$400,000
5	54	$20,000	$100,000	$98,211	$400,000	$104,887	$400,000
6	55	$0		$100,264	$400,000	$109,962	$400,000
7	56	$0		$102,314	$400,000	$115,242	$400,000
8	57	$0		$105,631	$262,215	$121,291	$305,298
9	58	$0		$109,029	$262,215	$127,651	$309,966
10	59	$0		$112,501	$262,215	$134,328	$314,840
11	60	$0		$116,043	$262,215	$141,251	$319,918
16	65	$0		$134,613	$262,215	$180,773	$348,158
21	70	$0		$154,521	$262,215	$230,286	$382,195
26	75	$0		$174,976	$262,215	$291,571	$423,653
31	80	$0		$194,972	$262,215	$365,827	$474,210
36	85	$0		$213,632	$262,215	$454,553	$534,734
41	90	$0		$228,213	$262,215	$557,295	$611,130

50 YEAR OLD MALE. GUARDIAN POLICY. $20,000/YR – 10 YEARS							
Age/Funding				GUARANTEED		CURRENT ASSUMPTIONS	
Yr	Age	Annual Outlay	Cum. Outlay	Cash Value	Death Benefit	Cash Value	Death Benefit
1	50	$20,000	$20,000	$17,269	$600,000	$17,269	$600,000
2	51	$20,000	$40,000	$36,462	$600,000	$37,294	$600,000
3	52	$20,000	$60,000	$55,469	$600,000	$57,752	$600,000
4	53	$20,000	$80,000	$75,144	$600,000	$79,787	$600,000
5	54	$20,000	$100,000	$95,513	$600,000	$102,996	$600,000
6	55	$20,000	$120,000	$116,614	$600,000	$127,472	$600,000
7	56	$20,000	$140,000	$138,475	$600,000	$153,308	$600,000
8	57	$20,000	$160,000	$161,122	$600,000	$180,591	$600,000
9	58	$20,000	$180,000	$184,588	$600,000	$209,446	$600,000
10	59	$20,000	$200,000	$208,881	$600,000	$239,968	$600,000
11	60	$0		$215,459	$486,857	$252,612	$561,218
16	65	$0		$249,938	$486,857	$324,905	$617,309
21	70	$0		$286,900	$486,857	$415,445	$683,137
26	75	$0		$324,880	$486,857	$527,668	$762,031
31	80	$0		$362,007	$486,857	$663,995	$857,373
36	85	$0		$396,652	$486,857	$827,257	$970,910
41	90	$0		$423,726	$486,857	$1,016,678	$1,113,476

It is not recommended that you ever close the policy because you will lose the death benefit and be required to pay taxes on anything above what you have contributed (cost basis). To learn more about the infinite banking and how to create your own Personal Bank check out the resources at personalbank4U.com.

Option 2: Conservative, Low-Risk, Low-Return Investments

If you are risk-averse, cannot take a 10% to 20% drop in the market, and you need your money to live on in the next five to seven years, then you should invest more in CDs, bonds and US treasuries. Do not put this money in bond mutual funds or ETFs because of their recent low returns and rising interest rates. The following are your better options:

Option 2a: Schwab money-market account (SWVXX) is a good interim place for your money while you are waiting to buy index funds. As of this writing, their 7-day yield is about 2.3%. These are not FDIC insured, but they are SIPC insured up to $500,000. This fund is available for individual retirement and investment accounts. If your account is a corporation, trust or 401(k), then you would use either the Schwab Government Money Fund (SWVXX) or the Schwab Treasury Obligations Money Fund (SNOXX), both currently returning about 2%.

Option 2b: Short-term treasury bills or notes and FDIC-insured CDs.
These investments are considered truly safe for those who do not want to take any risk and need funds available within the next five to seven years. When this book was written in April 2019, the daily treasury yield curve rates for six months was around 2.4%, and for one year the rates were about 2.6%, which barely keeps up with inflation. You can buy these online through treasurydirect.gov or through Charles Schwab and pay no commission. If you choose to work with one of the Schwab brokers, the trade will be $25. If you worry about fluctuations in the stock market, this is a good place to put your money. A Treasury Bill (T-Bill) is a short-term debt obligation backed by the Treasury Department of the US government that matures in less than one year. Other Treasury notes have maturities from two to ten years, while Treasury bonds have maturities of greater than 10 years. These both pay interest semi-annually, and the only real difference between Treasury notes and bonds is their maturity length. I recommend Treasuries over bond-exchange-traded funds (ETFs), because treasury bills are guaranteed. In 2018 the return for a one-year Treasury was more than 2% while the US bond fund was a −0.03%.

Option 3: S&P 500 or the total US stock market index mutual funds or ETFs—High Risk, High Return.
Because 80% to 90% of your total assets are in inflation adjusted assets such as your paid off home and business, Personal Bank and income, you can put 10% to 20% of your liquid assets into riskier assets such as index funds. To me, these two index funds are considered the gold standard of stock market investments, as they perform better than 96% of all other actively managed mutual funds. Warren Buffett has said that before he dies, he will put the inheritance for his children into a Vanguard S&P 500 fund and recommend they do not touch it. Buffett does not worry about economic analysis when

buying a stock or company. It is all about buying the right company at the right price and then holding that company forever. That is why he buys when the company or market is down (buy low).

My personal strategy is to keep most of my investing money in my Personal Bank with cash value earning near 5% and short term money in my Schwab money market account earning around 2% and wait to purchase my S&P 500 index fund when there is a 10% drop in the market. If the market drops further, I find more money to buy more. This is not trying to time the market and get in and out but just buying low when stocks are on sale. Once I buy these funds, I always keep them and do not sell. 2018 was a very volatile year for the market, which had a couple of more-than-10% drops in the S&P 500. Because I had funds stored in my money market account and Personal Bank, I was able to take advantage of the 10% to 20% drop and was rewarded with a 10% to 20% increase during the rebound in the S&P 500 index fund. Once I buy the S&P 500 index fund, I do not sell it but keep it forever and continue to add to my portfolio during these downturn opportunities (see table below).

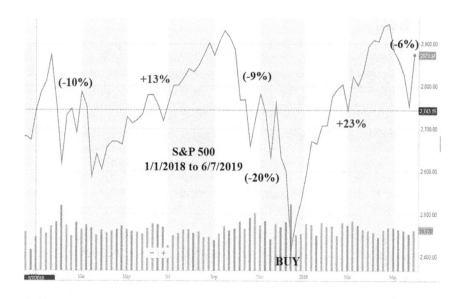

Both Vanguard and Schwab have both S&P 500 index mutual funds and ETFs with minimal fees. You can buy the Schwab S&P 500 index mutual fund (ticker symbol SWPPX) at the expense ratio of 0.03%, or the Vanguard

500 index mutual fund (ticker symbol VFIAX), with an expense ratio of 0.04%, both providing an average annual return over the past 10-year period of about 15.9% (see chart below). Or you can buy Schwab US Broad Total Market index mutual fund (ticker symbol SWTSX), at the expense ratio of 0.03%, or the Vanguard Total Stock Market Index ETF (ticker symbol VTI), with an expense ratio of 0.04%, both returning an average annual return over a 10-year period of 15.5%. The average 15-year return for both S&P 500 and the US stock market index was only 8.6% and 8.9% because of the 2008 market crash. These before tax returns are like the tax-free returns that you get in the Personal Bank (which also has a death benefit). The market can be volatile, and that is why I recommend most of your assets be in safe, inflation-adjusted, bond-like vehicles such as your paid-off home, paid-off business, steady income, and Personal Bank, with only 10% to 20% invested in your market gambling fund with the S&P 500 index or the total US stock market index. Then you're done—relax and enjoy life.

Comparing average annual returns for Schwab and Vanguard Index funds 4/1/2019 (Morningstar.com)								
	S&P 500 Index				Total US Stock Market Index			
	Vanguard S&P 500 MF	Vanguard S&P 500 ETF	Schwab S&P 500 MF	Schwab S&P 500 like ETF	Schwab Total US Stock MF	Schwab Total US Stock ETF	Vanguard Total US Stock MF	Vanguard Total US Stock ETF
Ticker symbol	**VFIAX**	**VOO**	**SWPPX**	**SCHX**	**SWTSX**	**SCHB**	**VTSAX**	**VTI**
Expense ratio	0.04%	0.04%	0.03%	0.03%	0.03%	0.03%	0.04%	0.04%
# of stocks	509	509	509	771	2728	2432	3680	3680
1 year	11.3%	11.3%	11.3%	11.3%	10.5%	10.7%	10.7%	10.8%
3 years	14.4%	14.4%	14.4%	14.6%	14.4%	14.5%	14.5%	14.5%
5 years	12.1%	12.1%	12.0%	12.0%	11.6%	11.7%	11.7%	11.6%
10 years	15.4%		15.3%		15.5%		15.5%	15.5%
15 years	8.6%		8.6%		8.9%		8.9%	8.9%

In 2017, I attended Berkshire Hathaway's annual meeting in Omaha, Nebraska. I sat about 70 feet from Warren Buffett when he told us about the bet he'd made with one of the large hedge-fund managers in 2007. He bet the fund manager of Protégé Partners $1 million, to be given to charity, that the

S&P 500 would beat a basket of hedge funds over the next decade. Warren Buffett looked out at the large crowd of 40,000 attendees and divided us in half. He said to those of us on the right side of the room that we were just average investors who could afford to put our money only in an index fund such as the S&P 500 and would settle for whatever it produced. But the 20,000 attendees on the left had a lot of available money; some were millionaires and could afford to pay 4.3% of their assets in fees to a hedge-fund manager and 3% to hedge-fund brokers each year to get extremely high returns. The fees paid to these hedge funds would average $98 billion a year.

Ten years after that bet, in 2017, the S&P 500 index fund had compounded an annual gain of 8.5% over the 10 years, beating the average increase of 2.4% earned by the basket of funds selected by Protégé Partners. This is another example of keeping it simple and staying away from high fees.

Remember to Stop the Noise

I recommend that you start investing only when you are completely debt free, because paying off debt gives you the highest rate of return without risk or fees. As you create a business model, you will find all the abundance that you need and will never think about so-called "retirement." Continue to invest each month in your Personal Bank, and add to your stock portfolio when you see a greater-than-10% drop in the market—this is the best time to buy. And never get out of the market during these drops. A YouTube clip from the classic television series *Bob Newhart,* "Stop it," reminds us to stop our negative self-talk, worries and anxieties over investing and what's happening in the market. Stop listening to the financial news, and focus on living and enjoying life. If you want true peace, stop listening to all the news. Once you have implemented *Dr. Ace's Financial Freedom Guide*, you can focus your energies on what you love, including the people in your life.

CHAPTER 7*

Enjoy Life, Liberty and the Pursuit of Happiness

The Most Important Chapter

Enjoying Good Health

About three years ago, I noticed that my computer IT guy had lost a considerable amount of weight. He was six foot two, and when I first met him, he weighed around 300 pounds. Within six months, he had dropped 100 pounds and now looked great. I was amazed because I disliked exercise and had always had trouble losing weight, so I asked him what his secret was.

He told me that weight loss was pretty much 90% diet and 10% exercise. He said he changed his eating habits and moved to a high-fat, low-carbohydrate, ketogenic method of eating. He recommended a site called Dietdoctor.com, which was founded in 2011 and has more than 55,000 members worldwide, making it the largest low-carb site in the world. It is filled with many articles, experts, videos and low-carb recipes.

At that time, I was five foot six and weighed about 200 pounds, with a beautiful pot belly. Within three months of taking his advice, I lost more than thirty-five pounds and have maintained my weight at 165 pounds for the past three years. I walk a couple of miles once a week and do some weightlifting two times a week to keep my muscle tone. I take multivitamins, vitamin D, magnesium, and fish oil. I can now sleep eight hours a night, and I feel better than I have for years.

Another great website to help transform your health is http://drhyman .com/. Dr. Mark Hyman is an American physician and a *New York Times* bestselling author. He is the founder and medical director of the Ultra Wellness Center and director of the Cleveland Clinical Center for Functional Medicine. His books and audios on understanding functional medicine can change your life. See Appendix A.

Creating Great Relationships

Warren Buffett gives the following advice: *"Be around people that you admire and enjoy. They usually have an upbeat attitude about life, they're humorous, have integrity and are generous people who are thinking about what they can do for you. These qualities that you admire are not innate at birth, and you can acquire them. Then there are those negative qualities that turn you off in people who always need to be right and that you don't enjoy being with. You can choose what person you want to be, so why not choose the person you admire? Take your five best friends, mentors or your heroes, and write down the qualities that you like about them. Incorporate these qualities in your life, and eliminate the qualities of the people that turn you off. It's that simple. It is important to work with people in your life, and you will get the best out of people if they like you. You need to develop these habits now. Incorporate the great qualities now and eliminate the bad qualities, and you will have an incredible life. Choose your heroes very carefully because they will define you. You are one of your children's favorite heroes."*

Buffett also said that the secret to long-lasting relationships is low expectations. A friend told me that relationships improved immensely when you give up the need to be right. My wife, Nancy, and I were married in 1969. We have five children and thirteen grandchildren. We have had our ups and downs, but we are very supportive of each other. And if she has a problem that I know I can fix immediately, I listen intently and never offer advice. (There is a great and funny YouTube clip called *"It's Not About the Nail"* that makes this point very clear.)

Another great book is *The Five Love Languages,* by Gary Chapman. The five love languages are words of positive affirmation, acts of service, receiving gifts, quality time and physical touch. Because I was abandoned as a child, my language is positive affirmation. This will fill up my love tank, while criticism will empty it. Even though I do some stupid things sometimes, Nancy is not critical of my errors. My wife's love language is quality time and acts of service. If she has something for me to do, such as change the burned-out light bulb in the kitchen, I immediately do it.

When I see my underwear drawer full, I know she did the laundry, and I thank her. I often tell her how beautiful she is and how much I love her. Even though our children may do things that we do not like, we provide advice only when asked, are never judgmental or critical, and are there to love them no matter what happens in their lives. Warren Buffett said he never met a truly successful person who did not have a great relationship with their children. Are you truly successful?

One last comment: I would never be in a relationship that is toxic or does not add true meaning to my life. Sadly, this toxicity could be from parents who are always judgmental and critical of you. Tell any toxic person that if they continue to be judgmental or critical, you will not be seeing them. I give you permission to take care of yourself first, or else you will not be good to anyone else. Think about what you are teaching your children about the type of relationship they should be in.

Creating love in your life

Love is that special feeling we get when we have a connection with people and things in our life. It is created when we initiate and give love to people and things. Somebody could love us, and yet we may not feel anything. But we always feel love when we are loving others. This doesn't apply only to loving people but also to things in our lives such as a good movie, a book, a special mug and other things we go back to and create that feeling of love. Like the movie, "Love Actually" is all around us.

Learning and Understanding Meditation

Meditation helps reduce your stress, increase your energy, clear your brain and relax the body for a deeper more restful sleep. It makes you feel more connected, less anxious, and helps you to be calmer and more clear-headed in demanding situations. It can help you experience better relationships and sharpens your life focus. To learn a simple and powerful form of meditation, I recommend the new book written by Emily Fletcher entitled, *Stress Less, Accomplish More: Meditation for Extraordinary Performance*. For a better understanding of the Zeva Technique of meditation, check out her website: https://zivameditation.com/online/ or watch her YouTube video https://www .youtube.com/watch?v=yy6uO0MzbPg.

Letting Go of Issues and Emotional Pain From Your Past

When I was three years old my mother divorced my father and he moved to another city. My mother had to go back to school to get her degree and my brothers and I lived with my grandmother for the next five years. At that young age I subconsciously blamed myself for their divorce because if I could had been a better little boy this would not have happened. I carried this shame and pain through adulthood hoping that no one would find out how bad I was. I subconsciously stuffed this emotional pain and started to feel from my brain, not my heart, where there was no pain. This inability to feel deep emotions affected many in my personal and business relationships. I can easily understand why many men are not emotional. Once I addressed these issues and let go of much of my emotional pain, which we can be easily done with proper techniques, my life and myself became more emotionally alive and peaceful. Many people carry deeply embedded emotional pain from their past that affects and controls their lives. This could be from abandonment (divorce), which I experienced, sexual abuse, not being wanted and there are many more. One group I worked with who are exceptionally good in helping individuals to identify, address and let go of these issues is Legacy Life Consulting. Contact them at: https://www.legacylifeconsulting.com/ David Stamation (208) 946-3894.

You Need to Take Care of Yourself First

Many people have been taught that to serve others they need to give away all their time and energies first before they take care of themselves, leaving them feeling exhausted, frustrated and angry. This is especially true with women. This is very sad. The fact is, you can better serve and help others if you take care of your own needs first. Taking care of yourself is the least selfish thing you can do. You cannot pour from the empty cup. You need to set time aside every day to love and nurture yourself resulting in you feeling happier and less resentful as you serve others. The magic word that you need to use more often is "No", I cannot do that, thanks for asking.

Teaching Your Children about Finances

Mahatma Gandhi was asked what his message to the world was. He said, "My life is my message." Teach your children the satisfaction of being a saver instead of a spender. You need to show them the satisfaction of accomplishment and doing a job well. Be the example for them of how they can find fun and joy in everything they do, instead of teaching them duty, responsibility and that you must work hard for a living.

Teach your children to understand the ideas in this book. Help your children find a job so they can fund a Roth IRA. Schwab is a great place to put this money because there is no minimum to open an account, and there are no fees when trading among their funds and ETFs. Any money your child makes, you can match. When the children are old enough, age ten or eleven, teach them the simple investing approach found in this book. William Bernstein, in his book *The Investor's Manifesto,* suggests you set up a small portfolio with index funds in each child's name. Teach them how to file their account statements, log in and print out reports. Every quarter, set up an investment meeting with them, and discuss portfolio performance. The most important thing you can leave your heirs will not be cold, hard cash, but rather the ability to save, spend and invest prudently. Reward them with the dividends and half of the capital appreciation of their stock funds. Let them experience both the ups and downs of the market, and help them with their emotions, showing them stocks that just came on sale. Andrew Tobias, in Chapter 10 of his book *The Only Investment Guide You'll Ever Need*, has some great ideas on teaching your children about finances.

Finding Happiness

When we get to be between forty and fifty years old, our lives change. Many of us go through a clinical depression because we have lost the excitement of starting our careers or our business. Things may be going smoothly. The kids may be in college. But life changes, even if we don't want to admit it. We don't make changes in our work life anymore, and we don't care if it gets any better; we just hope it doesn't get any worse. Sometimes we take up hobbies instead of creating excitement in our work lives. As we reach midlife, it's time to realize that this is it; it's not going to get any better; it's all in our minds. We need to recognize this as an opportunity to go to work happy every day and to change our relationship to work so that it is fun. Life can be exciting if we let it be.

The future does not exist except in our imaginations; the past is merely a trace in our minds. The brain changes our recollections to fit our own convenience and purposes. This is also true with our work lives. Once we understand that we are working on a day-to-day basis, not a year-to-year basis, our attitudes and philosophies change, and, incidentally, we become more prosperous and have more fun.

I have consistently found that those who were happy while they were working are also happy during their retirement years. The opposite is also true: those who did not enjoy their work don't find any more happiness in retirement than they did while they were working.

The life and business coach Kendrick Mercer once had a fifty-year-old client from North Carolina. The client told him he had hated his work for the past twenty-five years. The worst problem was that he could not quit because he owed so much money. Kendrick told him he could set up his finances to be economically free in ten years, but he knew his client's problem was deeper than finances, so he asked him, "Once you reach financial freedom, what are you going to do?"

"I would first quit my practice," the client told him.

"Then what are you going to do?" Mercer asked.

"I am going to golf," he replied.

"Then what are you going to do?" Mercer asked.

He said, "I will buy a place on the beach and walk on the beach."

"Great," Mercer said. "Then what are you going to do?"

"Then I will watch TV and read books."

"Then what are you going to do?" Mercer asked him one more time.

He became sad and somber and said, "I will just walk on the beach some more."

"Great! What are you going to do then?"

He started to cry and said, "I'm going to die."

This is a pretty sad story. There was no real aliveness to this man, just a dead story. Mercer's fifty-year-old client was trying to get someplace instead of loving his life.

Mercer told him, "My job is to assist you in knowing that life is never going to be any better or worse than it is right now. It's just how you're looking at it. For you to go back and spend one more day losing your life for some future time which does not sound all that exciting will make your life a failure."

The client did not like hearing this, but he knew it was true. Mercer told him to go home and change his mind and outlook so he could enjoy dentistry again and appreciate his patients, his staff and all his relationships. If he did this and still did not enjoy dentistry, then he should quit, sell everything and do something with his life that he enjoyed.

The dentist did go back and created a new story for himself and his practice, and then he began to enjoy his practice. Kendrick coached him to slow down and sell some things to get rid of his debt. The client finally started to relax. Because life is lived in the present, it will truly never get any better or worse than it is this minute. It's all a matter of how we look at our experiences. This principle is the same for each one of us.

I have helped individuals become debt free and financially secure. Yet many tell me they are not happy. What I learned from Kendrick Mercer is that we carry many family imprints, negative emotional experiences such as abandonment or abuse, that make us feel that we are not worthy of happiness. We need to address these issues and let go of the loss and pain from the past. Sometimes, we need counseling to help us through this process.

One company that I have worked with which has helped me and my clients and their employees in identifying what holds them back from enjoying and finding peace in every aspect of their lives, resulting in more peace and happiness, is Legacy Life Consulting (http://legacylifeconsulting.com/).

It's Never Too Late

You may be in your 50s or even 60s and feel stuck in your practice or business, and in your life. Just like the story above, you can reassess your business and life, and make changes now. I've worked with many clients in their 50s and 60s, helping them through the process of making their business more efficient and fun while working fewer days. We also talked about getting rid of the junk in your life. Junk is defined as anything that does not add meaning to your life.

First, find out what your net worth is by writing down all your assets and debts. Look at your practice or business, and eliminate everything that does not make it fun. This may include employees who are negative and cause drama. Once you become much more profitable, you could decide to sell your practice or business and move to a different part of the country, where it may be warmer or where you can be closer to your children and work part time. When you clear your mind and are open to all possibilities, the choices become endless.

As you go through this process, make sure you have your spouse on board. The junk you want to eliminate may include the large boat you use only two to three weeks out of the year, but costs you $1000 in slip fees and maintenance each month. You may have had a loss in an individual investment such as a stock or limited partnership. Realize that you already have taken the loss and that chances are great that it will never come back. However, your keeping this loss distracts you from moving on and learning from your lesson. So just sell it, and use the loss to offset your gains in other investments. The only exception are stocks that drop during a down market, because you should *never* sell in a down market. You may have rental property that causes you a lot of headaches and produces low financial returns. It may be the large house with high maintenance costs which you could sell and move into a new or smaller home or condo and invest the difference in your retirement account. Go through your closet, and get rid of all clothes and shoes that you have not worn in the past year. Check out Marie Kondo on Netflix or go to their website: https://konmari.com/. Getting rid of junk in your life gives you great peace of mind and contentment. Now you can focus on creating strong relationships with your spouse and your children.

What Percentage of Your Current Income Do You Need in Retirement?

Many financial advisors tell you that you need 70% of your current income to be comfortable in retirement. I think one reason they say this is to make sure you keep investing more money in their actively managed funds. You will probably need only between 25% and 35% of your current income. Let me summarize and do the math: Take your current income—let's say $120,000.

Subtract out 20% for taxes and 20% for retirement, and you're down to $72,000.

Subtract out 5% for insurance, 5% for child-related costs, and 15% for your mortgage. You're now down to $42,000. Subtract out another 1% for job-related expenses, 2% for reduced charitable contributions, and 1% for reduced housing expenses. You're down to $37,200. Add back in, say, 10%

for increased travel costs and 5% for increased healthcare costs. This moves us up to $55,200. Subtract out $36,000 for Social Security, and that leaves us at $19,200, or 16% of our current income.

The Illusion That Money Will Make Us Happy

Most Americans fall prey to the illusion that money will make us happy. There are more miserable, depressed, and anxious millionaires than you can imagine! I've seen clearly and repeatedly that money will *not* buy happiness. Nothing that money can buy will make you happy on an ongoing basis, and many people resent those who have money. This attitude will prevent them from creating abundance in their lives.

The belief that money will make us happy seems almost unstoppable. It is one of the big illusions that keeps us from developing integrity with money. Some people think that, if they win the lottery, they will be happy, but things never seem to work out that way. Money can make people miserable because of their false expectation of what it will bring. What makes us happy is having integrity in every aspect of our lives, including expressing our feelings through travel, love and relationships.

On some level, we all know money will not make us happy, but we still act *as if* it will. Money does bring a certain kind of security that we wouldn't otherwise have. With that security, perhaps we can express happiness or enjoy life more consistently. Being financially secure is different from being rich.

Happiness comes from enjoying each moment and appreciating everything that comes into our lives. It comes from helping others. This is where the real fun is. As we give love to others, we can't stop the abundance of love that comes into our own lives.

No precise dollar amount translates into this capacity. On the other hand, poor money management (such as having high debt and many creditors) can make you unhappy, and that is one good reason for developing a clear financial context. Sometimes it takes buying the things you always thought you wanted for you to realize that they alone do not bring you happiness. Spending without a clear guide diffuses and wastes your money and your financial freedom. If you have a clear context about money, you'll *rent* the boat or vacation home you've dreamed of first, to see if it really does add meaning to your life.

Jonathan Clements, in his must-read book *The Little Book of Main Street Money: 21 Simple Truths That Help Real People Make Real Money,* says that buying things might bring us happiness but not long-lasting happiness. Over the past decades, we, as a society, have made vast improvements in our standard of living, yet people still aren't any happier. We need to get off the treadmill and think about how we spend our money and how we spend our time. Clements makes six recommendations for happiness.

✓ Buy experiences rather than things.

✓ Count your blessings.

✓ Strive for a sense of control.

✓ Find a purpose instead of trying to create endless leisure time.

✓ Give a little, volunteer or donate.

✓ Make time for friends and family.

There is a wealth of information on his website, which is always updated and worth visiting. https://humbledollar.com/money-guide/main-menu/

Stop Complaining

Half of the people think you deserve what you get, and the other half don't care. Kendrick Mercer shared a story with me after his three-month sailing from California to Lahaina, Maui. His trip was an incredible adventure, with beautiful sunny days, stormy weather, moonbows at night and wonderful solitude. After arriving in Lahaina, he took a plane to Honolulu. He was enjoying the view over the ocean while a lady sitting next to him was complaining to him about her life, children and husband. During the break in her conversation, he looked at her and said, "Let's play a game. Let's pretend the plane breaks right in half, and we are all going to die. All you see in front of you is blue sky. We have two choices: we can grab on to the armrest in terror and think about all the things we didn't do in our life, or we can calmly unbuckle our seatbelts, stand up, jump forward, and fly for the rest of our lives." She did not say much after that but gave him a big hug at the end of the flight. Why not live our life in gratitude and enjoy every moment?

Cultural and Family Imprinting

I realized that, before my clients could be at peace with money, they had to open and address the deeper behavioral issues keeping them from having integrity with money and with life.

Our attitudes toward money can keep us from living full and peaceful lives. We have all inherited a range of imprints from our families of origin concerning money. These imprints often include prejudices, insecurities and false assumptions, which pull us away from developing integrity with money. We tend to repeat the clichés about money that we learned as children, even if they're not true, such as "You can never have enough money," "It takes money to make money," "The poor working man can never get ahead" and "You must work hard for your money."

Most people who have plenty of money keep working, not because they enjoy it or choose to, but because working has come to represent worthiness. It is a kind of cultural fad. Work seems to justify our very right to exist. Your family imprint for duty, responsibility and working hard for a living may be incredibly strong, or perhaps work has become an addiction. Many people work because that is what society expects them to do, or because their parents told them they'd be bums if they didn't work hard six days a week. Our current attitudes about money tend to limit our choices, even when we have achieved wealth. The ideal balance would be to have a great deal of money and at the same time to be at peace, doing only what we really want to do. For most of us, our lives are half over, and it is time to have some fun now! You cannot create what you cannot envision. Get very clear about making your life fun and enjoyable: feel it, and keep moving toward that vision. Bring your vision to your office and your family. Don't settle for anything less. Take time to talk to your children, not about duty or responsibility, but about what brings happiness, fun and joy into their lives and what it will take to create that story for them.

How Do We Define Success?

This can be different for each one of us. For me, it is about loving what I do each day, being at peace in my life, being in good health, having time to be with and enjoy the people I love, being debt free, having enough money that I don't worry about money anymore and having the time and resources to make a difference in the world around me. Others may define success as being the best businessman, making a lot of money, having time to do missionary work, retiring at age fifty-five, having $2 million in the bank—the list goes on. This book is not meant to define your success but to show you how to have enough time and money to make choices in your life that are right for you. *It's not about making a living. It's about making a life worth living.*

French writer François-René de Chateaubriand (1768 to 1848) said, *"A master in the art of living draws no sharp distinction between his work and his play; his labor and his leisure; his mind and his body; his education and his recreation. He hardly knows which is which; he simply pursues his vision of excellence through whatever he is doing, and leaves others to determine whether he is working or playing. To himself, he always appears to be doing both."*

How Much Is Enough?

If you are like most people in the world, one bowl of rice a day would be enough. Here in America, we think in terms of economic freedom. In my past book *Time and Money,* I define economic freedom as the day you have accumulated enough safe, liquid assets that can reproduce your lifestyle income (the amount of money it takes to maintain your lifestyle), with safeguards against inflation, for the rest of your life, without touching the principal. This will vary by individual, but once you are debt free, you could reach that point in five to seven years, simply by following the recommendations in this book.

Make a Difference in the World

There is a difference between success and significance. One of the great advantages of having more time and more money is the ability to make a difference in the lives of people in the world around us. One reason I enjoy going into the office two days a week is that I can create abundance to share with others. Each year, I donate to many great causes, including the Union Gospel Mission dental clinic for our street people, Safe Place for battered women, the food banks, a dental assisting program, my church and various other causes that make a difference in the world around me. I believe that this brings even more abundance into my life. Even though you are working on paying off debt, donate either your time or money to an important cause. This will make a difference in your life and those you help.

The Two-Dollar-Bill Story of Happiness

I love giving out two-dollar bills as a reminder of our freedom in the United States. The $2 bill is the only piece of US currency that depicts the same person on the front and on the back. On the front of the bill, we see Thomas Jefferson, the third president of the United States. Then we turn the bill over and see him signing the Declaration of Independence. The people standing around the table are the committee who wrote the declaration. The main author is Thomas Jefferson (the tall person in the center). The person standing on the far left is John Adams, the second president of the United States.

John Adams and Thomas Jefferson had a few things in common: They were both presidents and were the only presidents who signed the Declaration of Independence. They both died on July 4, within three hours of each other, exactly fifty years after they signed the Declaration of Independence.

Figure 8

In those days, the average man lived to age thirty-five. Adams was ninety, and Jefferson was eighty-three on the day they died. I believe the reason they lived two to three generations beyond the average man is that they were both highly motivated to instill and imprint the ideals of freedom and independence into our American culture. They lived with a purpose.

This is what makes the United States one of the freest countries in the world; we can work and live anywhere we want in this country. We are free to be in any mutual relationship we want and to leave it if it is toxic (a relationship where you will never grow and are always being put down).

Sadly, most Americans don't know they are free. Many feel trapped in their lives, business, jobs and relationships. They feel angry, controlled, frustrated, anxious or sad. These feelings come from a place of fear—many people fear change and have one foot in and one foot out of their choices (relationships or jobs). These feelings immediately disappear when the person acts, after choosing to change, or by putting "both feet in or out" of their choice.

The $2 bill reminds us of our choice to be free, independent and happy. The secret of happiness is in three choices. Any time you feel upset, angry or trapped, there is something in your life that you are not accepting. The courage to make one of these three choices will give you back your freedom and peace of mind. The choices are as follows:

1. You can change your situation (relationship or work), which takes courage as you face and conquer your fears. For example, if someone is always judgmental or critical of you and this is a deal-breaker, then you can tell them that behavior is no longer acceptable to you and that, if they continue, you will leave the relationship. If they stop this unacceptable behavior, then you will stay and be at peace. If not, you choose number two.

2. You can leave the situation (i.e., relationship or work).

3. If you can't change the situation or you choose not to leave the situation, then you can stay and accept the "what is" of the situation and be totally at peace with the situation because it is your choice. We need to change the question to: "why is this happening to me" to "why is this happening for me."

Summary

D r. Ace's financial freedom guide is very basic.

- First, write your new money story, and set your goals for increasing your income, eliminating your debt first and then increasing your savings and investments.

- Create a practice or business you love—one that is profitable—and then do more of it. Many business owners I coach complain about some of the people they work with who make them miserable. I tell them to go back to their office and tell the owner to fire those people. Then I remind them that *they are the owner.* Most people forget that they can make their business exactly what they want it to be. They have the canvas and the brush.

- Learn to make more money, and focus that money toward debt reduction. Once you are debt free, you should consider creating your own Personal Bank. To learn more about infinite banking and how to create your own Personal Bank, check out the resources at personalbank4U.com. You can put any excess money into a Schwab money market account and take advantage of 10% or greater drops in the market, as occurred in 2018. Learn to invest on your own in a Schwab or Vanguard account in the United States market through index funds such as the S&P 500 or total

US stock market. Once you feel comfortable investing on your own, share your knowledge and this book with other colleagues.

- Stop listening to the news and worrying about what's happening in the market. This is just noise. That's it. Now, enjoy your life, be grateful, and spend the rest of your money on things that add meaning to your life. This leads to financial freedom and a life of self-integrity and peace.

- Economic peace of mind is more than just financial freedom. In fact, we can experience economic peace of mind long before we reach financial freedom. *Once we have a solid guide in place for achieving financial freedom, we can let go of our anxiety about money and live as if it has already happened.* With this newfound peace of mind, we can truly enjoy life in the moment because we are secure in what we have, and we know that we can deal with any life challenge.

We can face life with joy and excitement once we have a vision and a beautiful story for our lives. With this book, each of us can claim both financial freedom *and* economic and personal peace of mind. "Being happy is a choice."

Acknowledgments

To my wife, Nancy, who has always been supportive of my adventures and misadventures while creating an incredible life for myself and our children.

To my father, who showed me the problems with gambling and spending recklessly and died broke at age sixty-five. To my mother, who understood getting out of debt early, saving and investing safely, and who retired a millionaire, living to be eighty-seven.

To my financial mentors,

Kendrick Mercer, my co-author on my last book, who taught me "If you have it made, why risk it?" More importantly, he taught me how to live my life in peace and contentment.

John Cummuta, who trained me on the importance of debt reduction.

Daniel R. Solin, who taught me the simplicity of just buying the S&P 500 index.

William Bernstein, whose down-to-earth investment books help me clarify my investment strategy through his humor and common-sense approach.

Warren Buffett, who has been an example of loving your work and living a great and simple life, and who taught me the importance of buying stocks on sale and keeping the investments forever.

Ben Franklin, one of our nation's founding fathers, who exemplified living frugally until you are out of debt and creating prosperity through hard work and sound business principles. He is the author of *The Way to Wealth*.

To all those stupid financial mistakes I made, which caused me great pain but at the same time taught me important lessons I remember well enough to share with you now.

To my athletic coaches (Mr. Bill Granger, Mr. Dick Truman, and Mr. Ralph Maughan), who taught me the importance of compassion and commitment of time and energy needed to help a person reach their highest potential.

To my twenty-year Army experience, which helped mold my leadership skills and revealed the importance of empowering people.

To Alex Nottingham and Trish Farrell, Drs. Mike Abernathy, Jim Kulild, Hugh Habas and Doug Carlsen, who thoroughly reviewed my rough draft and gave me valuable insights and made important corrections.

To my publisher and their editors, who helped make this possible.

Appendix A

Resources from Dr. Ace

Alexander, Michael A. *Stock Cycles: Why Stocks Won't Beat Money Markets Over the Next Twenty Years.* Writers Club Press, 2000.

Bernstein, William J. *If You Can: How Millennials Can Get Rich Slowly.* William J. Bernstein, 2014.

Bernstein, William J. *The Four Pillars of Investing: Lessons for Building a Winning Portfolio.* McGraw Hill, 2010.

Bernstein, William J. *The Investor's Manifesto: Preparing for Prosperity, Armageddon, and Everything in Between.* John Wiley and Sons, Hoboken, NJ, 2010.

Bogle, John C. *The Little Book of Common Sense Investing: The Only Way to Guarantee Your Fair Share of Stock Market Returns.* Wiley, Hoboken, NJ, 2017.

Burnell, Dwayne. *Path to Financial Peace of Mind* Paperback. Bothell, WA. 2010

Chapman, Gary D. *The Five Love Languages: How to Express Heartfelt Commitment to Your Mate.* Thorndike Press, Waterville, ME, 2005.

Clements, Jonathan. *The Little Book of Main Street Money: 21 Simple Truths That Help Real People Make Real Money.* LLC Gildan Media, 2009.

Clements, Jonathan. Website: https://humbledollar.com/money-guide/main-menu/

Cummuta, John M. *Turn Your Debt into Wealth: A Proven System for Real Financial Freedom.* Simon & Schuster Audio, 2001.

Cummuta, John M. *The Banker's Secret to Permanent Family Wealth: Live Your Life…and Build Your Wealth…Using the Same Money.* The smartest wealth system, 2017.

Dahle, James M., MD. *The White Coat Investor: A Doctor's Guide to Personal Finance and Investing.* The White Coat Investor LLC, 2014.

Dahle, James M., MD. Website: https://www.whitecoatinvestor.com/

Fletcher, Emily, *Stress Less, Accomplish More: Meditation for Extraordinary Performance.* HarperCollins Publishers, New York, NY. 2019

Goerig, Albert C., and Mercer, Kendrick. *Time and Money: Your Guide to Economic Freedom.* ACG Press, Olympia, WA, 2004.

Hyman, Mark. *Food: What the Heck Should I Eat?* Little, Brown and Company, 2018.

Hyman, Mark. *The Five Forces of Wellness: The Ultra Prevention System for Living an Active, Age-Defying, Disease-Free Life* Audio CD. 2006.

Headley, Jason. "It's Not About the Nail." YouTube. May 22, 2013. https://www.youtube.com/watch?v=-4EDhdAHrOg.

Malkiel, Burton Gordon, and Ellis, Charles D. *The Elements of Investing: Easy Lessons for Every Investor.* Wiley, Hoboken, NJ, 2013.

Malkiel, Burton Gordon. *A Random Walk Down Wall Street: The Time-tested Strategy for Successful Investing.* W.W. Norton & Company, New York, 2016.

Nash, R. Nelson. *Becoming Your Own Banker: Unlock the Infinite Banking Concept.* Infinite Banking Concepts LLC, Birmingham, AL. 2009

Parisi, Steve. YouTube: Infinite Banking 101: Live Webinar #1. 2018

Parisi, Steve. YouTube: Infinite Banking 101: Live Webinar #22 | Back to the Basics of the IBC. 2019

Phillips, David T. *The Family Bank Strategy: How to create your own personal Tax-Free bank and protect your estate from creditors and predators.* 2015

Robbins, Anthony, and Mallouk, Peter. *Unshakeable: Your Financial Freedom Playbook.* New York: Simon & Schuster, 2017.

Solin, Daniel R. *The Smartest Investment Book You'll Ever Read: The Proven Way to Beat the "Pros" and Take Control of Your Financial Future.* Pedigree Books, New York, NY, 2010.

Solin, Daniel R. *The Smartest Money Book You'll Ever Read: Everything You Need to Know about Growing, Spending, and Enjoying Your Money.* Penguin Group, New York, NY 2011.

Solin, Daniel R. *The Smartest Retirement Book You'll Ever Read.* Penguin Group, New York, NY 2010.

Stanley, Thomas J. and Danko, William D. *Millionaire Next Door: The Surprising Secrets of America's Wealthy.* Taylor Trade Publishing, 2010.

Thompson, Jake, Money. Wealth. Life Insurance. How The Wealthy Use Life Insurance as a Tax-Free Personal Bank to Supercharge Their Savings. Real wealth financial, 2013.

Thompson, Joshua, The Simple Banking System: A Concise Look into Life Insurance As An Investment Tool. Becoming your own bank, 2019.

Tobias, Andrew. *The Only Investment Guide You'll Ever Need.* Second Mariners books edition, New York, 2016.

Wattles, Wallace. *The Science of Getting Rich.* April 1910.

Yellen, Pamela. *The Bank on yourself revolution. Fire your banker, bypass Wall Street, and take control of your own financial future.* Benbella Books, Inc. Dallas, TX. 2016.

Zweig, Jason. *Your Money and Your Brain: How the New Science of Neuroeconomics Can Help Make You Rich.* Simon and Schuster, New York, NY, 2007.

Appendix B

Setting Your Debt-elimination Plan in Motion

To come up with an effective strategy for eliminating debt, it's important to have a clear sense of your monthly expenses and to determine how many of these expenses are payments on specific debts. Personal-finance software programs such as Mint.com or Microsoft Money can help you greatly in organizing this information on your computer.

First, write down all debts that you owe, along with the minimum payment for each debt, from the smallest to the largest (see below). We start with the smallest debt because we want to see results quickly, which helps us to continue the plan. Take 10% to 20% of what you make, and set up automatic payment through your bank, starting with the smallest debt. Once that's paid off, move on to the next debt. Continue this until all debt is paid off. You can write a check each month for the extra payment, but automatic payments are much more effective. *Very important:* **All payments must be directed to the principal of the loan, not just to the loan. You will find an in-depth, step-by-step plan below.**

Save unexpected extra money, tax returns, bonuses and pay raises, and immediately use this "found money" to pay off your consumer debt. Look for areas in your expenses that you can reduce. Don't buy new cars. You can save thousands of dollars by buying a car that is two to five years old. You may want to consider taking a second job for a short period of time to help eliminate credit card debt. Some couples live on one salary and invest the other. Quality of life is found in our relationships, the experience and the detail—not in the number of possessions we own. We need less to live on when we move from a materialistic life to one that is more inspirational and spiritual.

Once you've made a commitment toward financial freedom and debt reduction, it's important to act by freeing up money from unnecessary expenditures. Change your spending habits, and use only cash, checks or debit card to buy things. Use the 48-hour rule. For any purchase greater than $100, wait 48 hours to see if you really want to purchase that product. Most times, you will not.

Give yourself a set amount to spend each month so you get the feeling of what this is like. As an experiment, don't do *any* shopping for one month except for food. You may go through an initial withdrawal period. Facing your fears will help you to become wealthy. The way to stop salespeople from trying to sell you something is to simply say, "I can't afford that." If they persist, simply repeat your answer.

While you're reducing expenditures, be sure not to make any major purchases, such as a new car or boat, remodeling or a new house. I have had many great boats in my life, but someone else always owned them. For most people, boats always require more money than the pleasure they produce. Another must-read is *The Only Investment Guide You'll Ever Need*, by Andrew Tobias. This is an excellent resource book with ideas on how to save, make more money and get the most out of your money.

Step-by-step debt-reduction plan

Act Today. Declaring that you are seriously committed to getting out of debt is the first step to achieving personal wealth. Go through the steps below. All forms can be downloaded from DoctorAce.com. Also check out the resource section for the debt-free millionaire program and the Smart wealth system.

1. Sit down with your significant other: Both of you must be on board, knowing that this will strengthen your relationship, eliminate stress around money and give you back your freedom. Then read this book together, and set time aside to do the following:

2. Add up your net worth, that is, everything you own, and then subtract everything you owe in the chart below.

Determine Your Net Worth				
Assets	**Amount**	**Liabilities**	**Amount**	
Personal Cash (Bank)				
Business Cash (Bank)				
Taxable investments (stocks)				
Tax-deferred investments (IRA/401[k])				
Personal Bank-High cash value whole life insurance				
Gold/Silver				
Other				
Real estate		How much is owed		
Main home		How much is owed		
Vacation homes		How much is owed		
Rental property		How much is owed		
Business building		How much is owed		
Business value		How much is owed		
Other Assets		How much is owed		
Automobiles/boat		How much is owed		
Personal property		How much is owed		
Pension (value = 20x yearly amt)		School loans		
Social Security (value = 20x yearly amount)		Credit card debt		
		Other debt		
Total assets $		Total liabilities $		
		Net worth $ (Assets Minus Liabilities)		

Write down your total household income.

Net income source (after taxes)	Earner A	Earner B
Salary (net, take-home pay)		
Part-time or self-employment income		
Home-based business income		
Investment income		
Social Security		
Pension		
Veteran's benefits		
Other		
Individual totals		
Total income of A and B		

3. **Reduce your monthly expenses.** List all your current monthly expenses in the "current" column below. In the "reduced" column, record the lowest amount you can reasonably spend on each item. Total up all "reduced" amounts at the bottom of column 3, and then subtract that amount from your total income. The resulting number is your maximum possible *found debt-reduction money.* Go through your credit card receipts and checkbook, and add up all your monthly expenses. Use the list below. See where you can eliminate or reduce certain expenses. Those in **bold letters** are some of the best places to look for found money.

Monthly expenses	Current	Reduced
Retirement-plan contributions		
Going out for lunch at work		
Dining out (other than work lunches)		
Groceries (use coupons)		
Telephone (including cell phone)		
Heating fuel		
Water/sewer		
Electricity		
Car cost (fuel and maintenance)		
Parking, tolls, etc. (car pool or bus)		
Car #1 payment		
Car #2 payment		
Insurance—automobile (higher deductibles)		
Insurance—health (higher deductibles)		
Insurance—home (umbrella insurance)		
Insurance—other		
Home-equity loan payment		
Re-finance home mortgage (walk away)		
Other loan payment		
Child care		
Cable or satellite TV		

Monthly expenses	Current	Reduced
Movies		
DVD rental		
Other entertainment		
Sports (golf, fishing, etc.)		
Health club		
Lawn maintenance		
Laundry and dry cleaning		
Pet food and care		
Subscriptions		
Online computer services		
Credit card payment		
Credit card payment		
Credit card payment		
Christmas gifts		
College education for children		
Private schools		
Emergency fund		
Other savings		
Total reduced monthly expenses =		

Total income minus reduced monthly expenses = _____
(this is your *found debt-reduction money* used to accelerate your debt
payments)

4. Develop a spending journal, and for a month, write down each purchase you make (except regularly scheduled bills). This includes incidentals such as coffee, parking and other items less than a dollar. Use mint.com or download from DoctorAce.com.

Date	Item purchased	Cash	Credit	Check	Amount

5. Use the debt-elimination approach (described below) to pay off all debts within seven to ten years. Read through the debt-elimination-approach description, and then fill out the debt form to see how long it will take you to pay off all debts by making a 10% or 20% payment toward debt each month. I am not a big fan of budgeting. If you are serious about getting out of debt, automatically take 10% or 20% out of your bank account each month as if it were a tax. Live on the rest. **Automation of the payments is the secret!** Filling out the form below will help you understand your financial goals.

Debt-elimination Worksheet

Identify your debts, and record them on the Debt-elimination Worksheet below (you can go to Doctorace.com and download the worksheet). First, pay all small debts (less than $10,000) starting with the smallest. This "small debt" category includes credit card debt, consumer debt, auto loan balances and small student loans. Start with the smallest debt (no matter how high or low the interest), and then use the money from your *debt-reduction savings account* to pay it off first, while continuing to make the minimum payments on your other debts.

At the beginning, it's important to get momentum and see that you are making progress, so don't worry about the respective interest rates now. If the high credit card interest rate on a larger debt bothers you, you can always call the company and successfully negotiate a lower rate or transfer your balance to another credit card company with a lower rate.

Once you have paid off the first debt, you'll feel a sense of empowerment. Paying off that debt frees up additional money, which you add to your savings. Use this increased savings to pay down the next-smallest debt. Fill out the worksheet in pencil so that you can update it each month. This will help you keep on track and stay motivated.

As you pay down debt, you gain momentum and free up more money to pay off the next debt. The money that pays off these debts comes from increased income, reduced spending, and the extra money that becomes available as you pay off each debt. If you have money saved when you begin setting in motion *Dr. Ace's Financial Freedom Guide,* for the sake of your peace of mind, do *not* use that money for early debt reduction for at least six months. Below is an example of how we pay off debt.

First, determine what percentage of income you want to pay toward debt. If you and your spouse's average income is $72,000, you would divide this by 12 months, giving you $6,000; after taxes, that would be $5,000. 10% of this would be $500 per month.

The $500 (10%) will be paid each month to the principal of the top loan in the chart. First, add the $500 to the VISA card $30 payment, giving you $530 per month to pay toward that loan, which will be paid off in two months. When the VISA card is paid off, apply that $530 plus $32 to the next MasterCard loan, which will result in $562; it will take three months to pay off *that* loan. Your efforts will continue to eliminate all your debt. The debts will be paid off in seven years and four months, and you will have an extra $31,176 per year to invest, save, take vacations, send children through college or work less.

$500 (10%) Paid Monthly to the Principal of Top Loan in the Chart

Name of Debt	Total Balance (smallest to largest)	Monthly Payment	Accelerated Monthly Payment	Months to pay off
VISA Card	$1,000	$30	$530	2
MasterCard	$1,500	$32	$562	3
Department store	$2,000	$36	$598	4
Car 1	$9,200	$520	$1,118	9
Car 2	$14,300	$750	$1,868	8
Home-equity loan	$26,000	$370	$2,238	12
Mortgage at 4.5%	$155,000	$860	$3,098	50
Totals	$209,000	$2,598 ($31,176/yr.)		88 months (7 yrs. 4 mo.)

$1,000 (20%) Paid Monthly to the Principal of Top Loan in the Chart

Name of Debt	Total Balance (smallest to largest)	Monthly Payment	Accelerated Monthly Payment	Months to pay off
VISA Card	$1,000	$30	$1,030	1
MasterCard	$1,500	$32	$1,062	2
Department store	$2,000	$36	$1,098	2
Car 1	$9,200	$520	$1,618	6
Car 2	$14,300	$750	$2,368	6
Home-equity loan	$26,000	$370	$2,738	10
Mortgage at 4.5%	$155,000	$860	$3,098	43
Totals	$209,000	$2,598 ($31,176/yr.)		70 months (5 yrs. 7 mo.)

Your Debt-elimination Worksheet: Calculate Paying Off Your Debt
(Annual household income: $ _____)
(Average American debt is 2.5 times the annual household income)

1. Determine your extra monthly payments: $ _____

Try for 10% or more of your monthly take-home income. If you have only a home mortgage, then you should add 20% to 30% of your monthly take-home income.

2. Write down each debt in the first column below, prioritizing each debt from smallest to largest. Do not be concerned about the interest rate.

3. Using the debt-elimination approach, add your accelerator margin to the smallest debt, making this new monthly payment. Put this in column 4. To determine when the debt will be paid off, divide this amount into the total balance of that debt by the new monthly payment in column 4, and put the number of months to pay off in column 5.

4. When this debt is paid off, add what used to be the monthly payment amount to the next smallest debt payment, and place that in column 4. Again, divide this amount into the total balance of that debt by your new monthly payment in column 4. Put the number of months to pay off in column 5.

5. Continue adding each paid-off debt's monthly payment amount to its accelerated monthly payment and rolling the total amount to the next debt.

6. Add up the months in column 5 to determine when all debts will be paid off.

Name of Debt	Total Balance	Monthly Payment	Accelerated Monthly Payment	Months to Pay Off
1	2	3	4	5
Totals				

Things to keep in mind about your debt-elimination plan:

- Use only minimum payments to maximize the debt-elimination process.

- Use only the principal and interest portion of your mortgage payment (not tax/insurance).

- Interest rates are not a big factor.

- Only non-recurring debts go into your debt-elimination plan.

7. Write and post your Financial Goals. I am taking 10% of my income and paying off my debts. In six months (date), I will use 20% of my income toward an extra payment on my debts. I will pay off all credit card debt in one year (date), my car in two years (date) and my home in six years (date). Each month, review and challenge yourself to increase your debt reduction.

8. Develop a support group of either family or coworkers. Most families' money issues cause the greatest stress, and most do not understand how debt can keep a person in prison and take two thirds of their income throughout their lifetime. In my office, I created and presented to my team and their spouse a debt-reduction plan, which you will find at DoctorAce.com. In this program I showed them how to pay off debt, including their home, within 10 years, thereby freeing up more money to invest in their retirement fund. I also showed them how to invest safely with little risk and higher returns. Within six years, I have four of my employees completely out of debt, including their home, and the others have a game plan to be debt free within the next 10 years. Lisa and her husband are an example, below.

The greatest gift that I gave them is not being out of debt; the greatest gift is that I changed them from spenders to savers. This has done much to eliminate the money issues that many families argue about. The only drawback to this plan is that three out of the four team members who are now out of debt did not need to work as much and either now work part time in my practice or left the practice to enjoy their hobbies, which can be profitable. I just bring more people in and get them out of debt. Here is an example of one of those team members.

Lisa's Story

Lisa was my chief clinical dental assistant and was incredible at her job. She had a hobby selling things on eBay. Surprisingly, she was making more than $50,000 a year in her hobby.

Her husband was making about $15 an hour on his physically demanding construction job. They decided to live on his income and focus everything she earned from their eBay business and her salary from my dental office toward debt reduction and paying off their houses. They owned two homes, and, within four years, they had paid off their mortgage, sold one of the homes, and invested the profits into her company. Once debt free, they can open their own Personal Bank and put in $30,000 per year and at age 65 will have over $1,333,462 in cash value and a death benefit of over $2.6 million. They will use the cash value for their business and life purchases.

Lisa has since left my dental practice. She and her husband work about fifteen to twenty hours a week on their eBay business and have plenty of time for travel and enjoying the adventures of life. They had their first child in November. It is surprising how, with strong intent, becoming debt free happens very quickly.

9. Continue to read books such as those found in this book's references section, and listen to audios about debt reduction, including the ones found at DoctorAce.com.

10. Become the teacher. First set up and start the program yourself. Bring your family and friends together and watch these videos. Pass out the handouts, and help them set up the program for themselves. Share other debt-reduction resources with them. Share this material within your community, and help them regain their freedom.

11. Celebrate Success. This is *not* a no-spending plan; it is a managed-spending plan. I am not saying you can't spend any money on the things you want… But I *do* want you to be aware of the impact that each expenditure has on your ability to build your wealth. Most people can easily spend and live on half the amount they normally spend.

Managing bumps in the road. If you have an emergency during this time— for example, major car repairs or unexpected medical bills—you can use your paid-off credit card or skip a month or two of debt-reduction payments and use the cash that would have gone toward debts to cover the emergency. The same is true if you feel you need an inexpensive vacation: skip a month or two of debt reduction, and pay for your vacation with cash. Just be sure to get back on track with your debt-reduction plan as soon as you can. I do *not* believe that you must have an emergency fund for you to start debt reduction. Some consultants recommend three to six months of income, but if you wait

for that, it might take you two or three years to start your debt-reduction program. Once you have a paid-off credit card, you *do* have an emergency fund.

Once you've made progress paying down your small debt, be sure to
fund your Roth IRA and any pension plan at work up to the limit that the
company matches your money.

As soon as you've paid off all your small debts (less than $10,000), cel-
ebrate! Now take the "found money" you have freed up, and use it to pay off
large debts (more than $10,000), such as your car loan, your home mortgage
and any lines of credit. This may seem like a slow process, but once you've
paid off all your debts and are regularly investing in your retirement funds,
you'll have a considerable amount of excess money left each month to invest in
the investment strategies described later in this book. By following this plan,
most people can pay off all their credit card debt in one year and their car in
the second year. By the third year, they are making extra payments toward
the principal on their mortgage. Most people following this plan can be debt
free and pay off their home in seven to ten years.

When your last debt (home) is paid off, 40% to 60% of your income
will be available for investments or to place into your savings. This will allow
you to become totally financially free in another eight or nine years. Figures 3
and 4 are examples of the debt-elimination approach to paying off your debts.

The Nine Principles of Investment and Debt

By following these Nine Principles, you can achieve financial freedom:

1. The key to financial freedom is to make more than you spend
    or spend less than you make.

2. Make sure that every asset, large and small, adds meaning to
    your life.

3. Your best source of money is your ability to earn it, not investing.

4. If you have it made, don't risk it. You now can save enough money
    to retire early if you just play it smart by putting your money in
    safe investments, as described in Chapter 4.

5. Because your best source of money is your ability to earn it, not in the stock market, focus on ways to increase your income: make yourself more valuable at your job, go back to school, or work part time until you become debt free.

6. No matter how much you make, always automatically take 10% to 20% and pay off your debts. Spend less than you make, or make more than you spend.

7. Keep only the material possessions that add meaning to your life, and get rid of the rest—it is just junk.

8. Purchasing a home is an effective use of debt. Although it is not a liquid asset, it adds meaning to your life. Homes have also proven to be good long-term investments and provide a hedge against inflation.

9. Always save for consumption; never borrow for consumer items, vacations and so forth. Pay off all credit cards and consumer debt in full each month.

About the Author

D r. Ace Goerig graduated from Case Western Reserve University Dental School in 1971. He spent 20 years in the US Army as a dentist and retired in 1991, attaining the rank of colonel. He has been in private practice for 28 years in Olympia, Washington. In 1996, he co-founded Endo Mastery, a coaching program to help doctors and their teams create personal and financial freedom in their lives.

In 2004, Dr. Goerig co-authored *Time and Money: Your Guide to Economic Freedom* with Kendrick Mercer. He has a free website, DoctorAce.com, with audios and videos to help individuals quickly become debt free and eventually financially free. He and his wife, Nancy, were married in 1969 and have five children and thirteen grandchildren.

Testimonials

"Everyone should keep this book bedside and read and re-read it. The advice is sound, easy to understand and implement. I consider Ace Goerig a combination of John Bogle and Warren Buffett for individuals who want a secure financial future."

— **Dan Solin,** Author of the *Smartest* series of investing books.

If you want to get the most out of your life, especially your financial life, you must read *Dr. Ace's Guide to Creating Your Personal and Financial Freedom.* In these pages you'll find the essence of what it takes to maximize your financial outcome. It's not really complicated…at least not the numbers part. Financial success is 90% psychology and 10% math. Once you understand what's being done to you financially, and by whom, you will do whatever it takes to implement the 10% math part. Dr. Ace helps you understand the psychology—your powerful motivation to follow through—by framing it into your story. Like every good story, there are allies and enemies, a hero and a villain. You are the hero of your story, and Dr. Ace clearly explains exactly how to defeat the financial villain and live happily ever after. Start rewriting your financial-life story today by reading this book.

— **John Cummuta,** national speaker and
author of *Turn Your Debt into Wealth*

Dr. Ace Goerig is a genius when it comes to unlocking the key to happiness in life! Ace's book outlines exactly what you can do to achieve this outrageous happiness in life. This book shows you how to pay down your debt quickly, while learning to love going to work because you "get to" rather than "have to." That, folks, is pure happiness.

> — **Linda Miles,** Founder/CEO Linda Miles & Associates;
> Founder, Speaking Consulting Network. Dental
> practice management consultant for 40 years.

Ace has created a blueprint that has been found tried and true thousands of times. You are fortunate that you don't have to reinvent the wheel or spend one more day struggling, only to find another strategy that does not work. This is a playbook for success in life in which Ace outlines a concise, consistent financial plan that works.

> — **Michael Abernathy DDS,** Founder of Summit Practice Solutions

A superb book! Dr. Goerig demonstrates the keys to happiness and financial success. The core of his message is to become financially free while enjoying your life. Money in and of itself will not make you happy, but having enough money not to worry about money allows you to develop your passions. Build enough wealth through conservative, proven investments, get out of debt, gain perspective, and then use most of your time cultivating a life that is real, a life based on what you want, not what your parents or society tells you to be. Follow his advice, all of it, and I assure you that you will be 1,000% better for it!

> — **Alex Nottingham, JD, MBA,** Founder &
> CEO of All-Star Dental Academy

Dr. Ace has a great way of exposing what's behind the curtain when it comes to personal finance. Most folks, unfortunately, take financial products at face value and rarely peel back the layers to discover the truth. Dr. Ace will help you peel back the layers so you can discover what path is best for YOU, not those who peddle financial products. If you're serious about getting your personal finances in the best fiscal shape so your financial future is as healthy as it can be, you need to read this book!

> — **Anthony Manganiello,** Author of *Great Credit
> for Life* and *The Debt-FREE Millionaire*

I've known Ace for 35 years, and he has always been focused on value, quality, self-improvement and mentoring others. This book is a continuation of those attributes and gives the reader the skills and knowledge to live a life of peace, joy, hope, contentment, achievement and financial freedom. By putting his principles into action, you will be able to claim "victory," and that success will spread to your office staff, your patients, and, most importantly, your family.

— **James C. Kulild, DDS, MS** Past President, American Association of Endodontists, Diplomate, American Board of Endodontics, Professor Emeritus, Department of Endodontics UMKC School of Dentistry

This book is one of the most comprehensive and compelling publications on the subject that I have experienced. Its uniqueness and what differentiates it from others is that it specifically addresses the lifelong needs and goals of individuals everywhere—issues and subject matter certainly not taught in our nation's schools. This book is a terrific read for all of us at any stage of our career, to and through retirement.

— **Hugh Habas DDS** New Jersey. National presenter on practice management.

Here it is in a wonderful, compact nutshell—the "crux" of the Ace Goerig philosophy of practice, personal finance and life boiled down to this beautiful game plan for happiness in our practice and personal life! Why "recreate the wheel" when you have the best practice-management mentor generously sharing his experiences and wisdom with us for a life filled with peace, joy and fulfillment? This book is a must-read for everyone and gives us life skills to share with our loved ones, too!

— **Richard C. Wittenauer, DDS,** diplomate, ABE, California